29 PRINCIPLES AND POWERS OF ATTRACTION

MAGNETIC GEMS FOR ACTIVATING, ENERGIZING, AND PROFITING FROM THE LAW OF ATTRACTION

Other books by Steven Claysen:

The Power of Attraction:
How to Apply the Law of Attraction to Create the Life You Want.

The Lehrman Project:
Experiments in Subconscious Communication.

29 Principles and Powers of Attraction

Magnetic Gems for Activating, Energizing, and Profiting from the Law of Attraction

By Steven Claysen

First Edition published 2021.

ISBN-13: 978-1-7342387-3-0
ISBN-10: 1-7342387-3-9

Green Stem Media
A DeepEnd Book

www.greenstemmedia.com

www.stevenclaysen.com

"WE ALL HAVE THE ABILITY TO DESIGN OUR OWN LIVES."

BOB PROCTOR

CONTENTS

Publisher's Note

Get More Out of This Book

Sterling Sill, author of over 30 books, once wrote about an article he read entitled *How to Get More Out of a Book Than There Is in It.* "Good readers," he explained, "may be able to get out of a book all there is in the book, but with a little imagination and some ability to analyze, they may get much more."

All capable readers can have their thoughts strike a particular notion, causing their thinking to drift away from the material they are reading. We should not be too quick to draw our minds back into the book, since frequently if we give our imagination a little freedom, it will direct us to some *interrelated* way of thinking that could prove to be extremely valuable.

People may often find that the most significant insights, ideas, and beliefs are the ones that they come up with on their own and not so much from the concepts printed on the page. As our mind wanders along its own specific chain of correlated thought, we may arrive all on our own at some important interpretations and impressive conclusions. Then, when our minds have finished their journey of exploration and discovery, we can return our attention to the book and resume reading.

This is how to get more out of a book than there is in it. The book will cause us to come to conclusions regarding a diversity of *notions not actually in the book*. The interest of freeing our thoughts is an extremely beneficial and rewarding undertaking.

Paul, the New Testament apostle, was a known ponderer. He advises us that "whatsoever things are true, whatsoever things are honest, whatsoever things are just, whatsoever things are pure, whatsoever things are lovely, whatsoever things are of good report . . . *think on these things.*"[1] The ability to ponder gives us the capacity to obtain more from our circumstances and situations than what is actually in them. Through this procedure we place ourselves above the conventional and commonplace existence.

Thousands of fantastic, fascinating philosophies are frittering away in countless books. Hundreds of important and profound programs that could benefit us immensely sit untouched on library shelves. Even the word of God Himself remains largely unfamiliar and unacquainted to many of us. All the essential ingredients for success in any of our personal pursuits cannot advance our progression until we ingest and

---

[1] Philippians 4:8.

absorb them; until we get them circulating in our bloodstream and make them a part of our inner strength and learning.

As you read this book, or any other, practice the art of pondering. It will give you a more prolific passion for learning and thinking and, hopefully, for putting into practice. If what you read here does not please and persuade you, so much the better. You can amend each gem or each chapter to your own specific situation to satisfy your own particular prerequisites.

Effective pondering will enable you to draw concrete conclusions and form compelling objectives on the vital subject of your personal progress in life. With this in mind, we have included a blank page at the end of each chapter with the heading: *Insight and Inspiration*. This page is where you can record your own thoughts, ideas, insight, or inspiration. Don't just copy the author's words; write down your own thoughts and get more out of this book than there is in it.

"ONLY BY MUCH SEARCHING AND MINING ARE GOLD AND DIAMONDS OBTAINED, AND MAN CAN FIND EVERY TRUTH CONNECTED WITH HIS BEING, IF HE WILL DIG DEEP INTO THE MINE OF HIS SOUL."

JAMES ALLEN

INTRODUCTION

I have had a lot of people tell me that the Law of Attraction doesn't work. Some have tried to use the Law of Attraction to achieve better health, greater wealth, increased opportunities, to develop personal relationships and a myriad of other desires. "It's a hoax," they tell me. "It simply doesn't work." Meanwhile, I am enjoying all the health, wealth, opportunities, and relationships I desire thanks to the Law of Attraction.

So, what am I doing differently that allows me to use this incredible gift from the Universe that others are not doing? How am I manifesting my desires while they are not? The more I have questioned others who say that the Law of Attraction is a fraud, the more I recognize that they don't quite grasp the operations of the subconscious mind or the Law of Attraction for the purpose of manifesting their desires.

A person who had never seen a car before would not understand all the different functions and unique operations of the mechanics that make the automobile useful to us. They would be unable to use the car to achieve the results that car owners enjoy daily. Such a person would have a powerful vehicle and everything they need at their disposal to manifest any desire in life. The problem subsists not with the vehicle, (that is, the Law of Attraction); the problem exists with the vehicle's operator. If we don't know how to 'drive' or operate the Law of Attraction, we can't expect to effectively use it to reach our goals, wants or desires.

The car analogy may be an overly simplistic description but for many people this embodies their experience using the Law of Attraction. Someone who is unfamiliar with the Law of Attraction may be told that they can attract anything they want into their life. They may believe that all they need to do is 'think about' what they want, and it will appear. Armed with this misinformation, they begin thinking about the things they desire in life, but nothing manifests itself and, consequently, they conclude that the Law of Attraction doesn't work, that the vehicle is defective.

What is actually occurring is not an issue with the vehicle but the lack of a clear knowledge and understanding regarding how the vehicle operates. Just like a car, there are many components that make up the Law of Attraction. Without an accurate concept of how the Law of Attraction operates, it isn't very likely that we will be able to effectively use it to achieve our desires. Once, however, we become familiar with the principles and powers of the Law of Attraction, we can then effectively use this magnificent vehicle to create whatever we desire in life. Without this knowledge and understanding, the vehicle remains idle and useless.

If you want to manifest something, the Law of Attraction is the vehicle that will help you realize your goals, dreams, and passions. But like a car, you can't just sit in it and expect miracles to happen.

29 Principles and Powers of Attraction is a type of Operator's Manual for directing the subconscious in the manoeuvring and management of the Law of Attraction. This book explains the required functions, the essential operations and the necessary skills involved in effectively producing positive results from sourcing the power of the Law of Attraction.

I have always hated the word 'secret' when used in the context of *Money Secrets of the Rich and Famous* or *Celebrity Weight Loss Secrets* published in magazines with a circulation of 30 million or more. That hardly sounds like a secret to me. I refer to the 29 powers and principles in this book not as secrets but as 29 *gems* for energizing, activating, and profiting from the Law of Attraction. This may seem like semantics to some but in his book, *As a Man Thinketh*, James Allen explains that: "Only by much searching and mining are gold and diamonds obtained, and man can find every truth connected with his being, if he will dig deep into the mine of his soul." [2] These 29 gems represent the indispensable, basic principles, and powers of operation essential to effectively energize, engage, direct, and accelerate you toward your dreams and desires.

---

[22] Allen, James. *As a Man Thinketh*, p. 15.

The following chapters contain a detailed description of the principles and powers which govern the Law of Attraction, an understanding of which will give us greater control in effectively operating this law and an increased ability to manifest our strongest desires.

A law is simply a theory that has been implemented, practiced, and proven over time to perform in a consistent manner. The Law of Attraction and the following principles and powers in this book have been applied and proven and can be considered established and consistent laws of manifestation and attraction. These powers and principles are available to anyone willing to implement them.

We may envy the success of others. We may desire similar wealth, happiness, or relationships without ever considering studying, imitating, and implementing their philosophies, habits or methodologies and appropriating them in our own processes. Study and ponder the material in the following short, simple chapters. Implement the principles and practice them. As you do, you will re-prove the laws that correspond to manifesting your desires through the Law of Attraction. You will begin to operate this vehicle effectively to drive and direct yourself to obtain all that you desire and to become all that you are meant to be. You will begin to use the Law of Attraction consciously rather than simply "sitting in the vehicle" hoping it takes you where you want to go in life.

Do not become too overwhelmed imagining that you must become an expert in implementing all 29 principles and powers at once. Each principle you practice and improve upon will bring you closer to manifesting your desires. The more principles you can put into practice, the more effective you will become at creating the life you desire quickly and effortlessly. Concentrate on developing one or two. As you become better with those, add a couple more. Work on the specific areas that *you* feel need more of your attention.

At the end of each 'gem' you will find a blank page entitled "Insight and Inspiration." Use these pages to jot down your thoughts and ideas as you read through each gem. Allow yourself to "dig deep into the mine of your soul;" that is where you will discover the riches of truth connected to your own being. These are the diamonds that will enrich your life and lead you to effectively manifest everything you desire. This is where you will write the words of wisdom that come from your own soul.

And, whatever else you do, enjoy the process.

"ONE OF THE KEYS TO MAKING THE LAW OF ATTRACTION WORK FOR YOU LIES IN KEEPING YOUR DESIRES AT THE FOREFRONT OF YOUR MIND, THUS GIVING THEM POSITIVE ATTENTION, ENERGY, AND FOCUS."

MICHAEL J. LOSIER

THE POWER OF DESIRE

The eastern American Black Walnut is a species of deciduous tree native to North America. The Black Walnut, with its deep brown wood, is a commercially important tree. The fruit of the Black Walnut is cultivated for its distinctive and desirable taste but getting the fruit out of the shell is an extremely difficult task.

The shell itself is thick and hard and is tightly bound to a dense husk. Breaking the shell requires rolling the nut under a hard-soled shoe against a solid surface such as a cement driveway. Commercially, huskers rotate a car tire against a metal mesh to separate the fruit from the shell. Of course, you could take a thick plywood board and drill a nut-sized hole in it and smash the nut through with a hammer. The nut goes through the hole while the husk remains behind.

The shells of these walnuts are so hard that they are often used as an abrasive in sand blasting and in scrubbers for smokestacks, cleaning jet engines and oil well drilling. In other words, they're hard!

And yet, when life inside the Black Walnut begins to stir, no impenetrable shell can stop it. The weak and vulnerable little plant inside breaks the stone-hard shell as if it were tissue paper. Life sends the tiny shoot up through the rich, dark soil toward the warm sun to eventually become a great Black Walnut tree.

Desire in the human heart and mind is like the force that exists inside the hard shell of a Black Walnut. Every principle and power in the Law of Attraction is secondary to desire. As James Allen stated: "To desire is to obtain; to aspire is to achieve." [3]

Former U.S. Senator Reed Smoot once stated that: "An ambition to excel is indispensable to success." Ambition is desire in action, but there is much more to desire than mere ambition.

Anything we desire strongly enough we are usually capable of achieving or manifesting. If we desire to become successful at something (you decide what that something is), then we are not that far from *becoming* successful at it. Our strong impulses, in this case, our desire, create a mysteriously powerful energy. When we combine a strong impulse with a determined resolve, we develop an energetic personality that assures our success in manifesting our most heartfelt dreams. Someone offered the idea that freedom from desire is one of

[3] Allen, James, *As a Man Thinketh*, p. 58.

the greatest freedoms. I would suggest that the freedom *to* desire is an even greater freedom.

Every vibration we unthinkingly emit or deliberately send out creates our future. Once we make decisions based on our sincere desires, we become even more intentional and conscious about the vibrations we give off. A thimble full of intelligence with a gallon of desire is so much more powerful than a gallon of intelligence with only a thimble of desire.

It is one thing to identify our desires; to write them out as goals or paste them up as pictures on a vision board. If we stop there, however, then our desires are doomed. We must also give positive energy to each of our desires every day. The more positive energy and focus we give to our desires and emotions, the more we increase our vibration. We develop a type of emotional autointoxication when we identify what makes us feel good or positive and then do more of it.

Desire is like the scent of blood on a tiger's nose; it inflames its appetite. Desire creates an aspect of self-hypnotism which turns fatigue into fascination and obstacles into opportunities. People rarely succeed at anything without a strong desire. It is an incredibly powerful principle when appropriately applied in our intention to manifest those things we are seeking in life.

Too many of us spend our lives as spectators rather than participants, missing out on creating the life we wish for. The powerful energy and momentum conceived by a strong desire is one of the greatest creative forces in the Universe.

Whatever you wish to create or manifest in your life, cultivate a powerful desire for it, contemplate its significance, magnify it in your own eyes, fan the small flame of desire until it becomes a raging forest fire.

And remember this important law of nature: *Whatever you desire with enough intensity, the Universe will wrap up and deliver it to you free of charge.*

Insight & Inspiration

"DREAM LOFTY DREAMS, AND AS YOU DREAM, SO SHALL YOU BECOME. YOUR VISION IS THE PROMISE OF WHAT YOU SHALL ONE DAY BE; YOUR IDEAL IS THE PROPHECY OF WHAT YOU SHALL AT LAST UNVEIL."

JAMES ALLEN

THE VISION PRINCIPLE

My wife works in the geology department of a major university. When we go traveling, I see a mountain; she sees the underlying tectonic process of geomorphology with its folding, faulting, volcanic activity, igneous intrusion and metamorphism that are part of the orogenic process of mountain building. I see a desert; she sees rock outcrops, exposed bedrock and clays once deposited by flowing water and now exposed to the weathering processes of large variations in temperature which break rocks into tiny fragments and rubble that are further eroded by the wind and end up as level sheets of sand or high billowing dunes.

An imposing mountain or vast desert contain so much that is visible to a geologist but that remains unseen to those of us whose minds lack the necessary knowledge or vision. In this way, we "have eyes but do not see."

One vital, key element necessary in activating and energizing the Law of Attraction is vision; the power to see beyond our current, temporal interpretation and assessment to the realization of everything we desire. It is all there; we just need to develop the ability to envision it and then manifest it. Frequently, we fail to see far enough or distinctly enough or promptly enough into our own future.

We usually think of the ability to see as a physical attribute, but vision is much more than a physical characteristic or quality. The eyes are merely instruments of sight. The most important feature of vision is in our outlook, perspective, and attitude. True sight exists in our judgment, our understanding, and in our imagination.

The Law of Attraction requires that we look openly and distinctly beyond the periphery of our present situation, circumstances, and surroundings. Imagine if the headlights on a car only illuminated a foot or so ahead of the vehicle. It wouldn't be unreasonable to expect disaster on some dark road at night. Likewise, a lack of vision in implementing the Law of Attraction promises future misfortunes.

Vision is light. The greater light we place on the object of our desire, the greater our ability to exert a pull on that object. Vision is an essential character-quality in manifestation and in effectively utilizing the Law of Attraction. The ability to look toward the future and to plan and act in accordance with our vision is one of the paramount components of human personality. The usefulness of the Law of Attraction is in direct proportion to the succinctness of our visualization and the span of our vision.

A blind man by the name of Bartimaeus sat at the edge of the road begging for his livelihood. He had begged and pleaded throughout his entire life for almost everything he owned. Certainly, by-passers had proffered him food, or money, maybe some had provided him with shelter for the night. I imagine that even the clothes he wore he obtained by begging for them. The items Bartimaeus acquired from others were essential for survival but held extraordinarily little material value. Then one day Bartimaeus heard that Jesus of Nazareth was coming down the road. The blind Bartimaeus called out to him. Jesus asked him: "What do you want me to do for you?" He could have asked anything of Jesus but Bartimaeus did not beg for some modest, ordinary gift. The blind beggar pleaded: "Rabbi, let me see again." [4]

When attempting to use the Law of Attraction, many suffer from short sightedness or internal blindness. Otherwise capable and talented people often cannot seem to see into the future to create a vision that exists beyond their current circumstances and list of wants and demands. This type of blindness jeopardizes and impairs the usefulness, effectiveness, and success of our ability to manifest our desires.

Our barrier to better vision can be illustrated with a simple visual illustration. If we hold a quarter out at about arm's length, it can completely obliterate our view of the sun.

---

[44] Mark 10:51.

And yet we know that the sun is so much bigger than that tiny coin. When we are walking along a country road, we may see a house off in the distance that seems extremely small, so much smaller than the house right next to us, and yet we are not duped into believing that the house in the distance is actually that small. Our brains and vision can adjust to this type of optical illusion where things in the distance appear small and insignificant.

Short sightedness can torment and trouble our efforts to manifest our desires. To effectively implement the Law of Attraction, we need to teach our minds to compensate for the illusion that objects in the distance appear small and unimportant. Our vision and our imagination can run ahead of us on the road of life to focus a spotlight on our future so that it stands out like a beacon to light our path toward the manifestation of our desired life. When we finally reach the horizon of our inner desires, we will understand how we have manifested our future life into the present day.

To manifest our desires in the present requires that we develop the ability to project our plans and hopes beyond the boundary of our present situation. Like in the illustration with the quarter and the sun, when our focus is singularly on the present, our future tends to be blotted out of our vision. When we lack vision, we generally live just day-to-day. Those people who have vision contemplate, prepare, and plan for the future they desire. Their vision can reach the stars and bring to them all the beauty and harmony of the Universe. The adage that "where there is no vision, the people perish" [5] is still true today.

Close your eyes and envision yourself living the life you desire. Imagine yourself there. What does it look like? How do you feel being there? What colors do you see? What scents surround you? Focus on all the details of your desired life. Now open your eyes and expect the Law of Attraction to draw your vision into existence.

Our imagination can transport us into the future so that we pre-live life's events prior to experiencing them. It combines circumstances with reason, hope, and belief to create an image of our future. This combination creates our vision. James Allen, author of *As a Man Thinketh*, tells us that "the greatest achievement was at first and for a time a dream. The oak sleeps in the acorn; the bird waits in the egg; and in the highest vision of the soul a waking angel stirs. Dreams are the seedlings of realities." [6]

Imagination is a major component of vision. The quality of our vision is enhanced by our dreams, our hopes, our determination, and by the image we hold of ourselves. Neville said that "all things are possible to you because you are all imagination and imagination creates reality. Knowing what you want, imagine you have it. Knowing what you want to be, imagine you are it."

To activate, energize, and profit from the Law of Attraction, we need to be clear and specific in our desires. The

[5] Proverbs 29:18
[6] Allen, James, *As a Man Thinketh*, p. 53.

Law of Attraction is always responding to our vibration, whether intended or unintended. It is imperative that we keep our focus off what we don't want and direct it continuously toward what we do want.

Vision says I see it.
Faith says I believe it.
Imagination says I will achieve it.

To profit completely from the Law of Attraction we need to be able to say, as did the blind man in the book of John, "although I was blind, now I can see." [7]

---

[7] John 9:25.

Insight & Inspiration

"UNITL THOUGHT IS LINKED WITH PURPOSE, THERE IS NO INTELLIGENT ACCOMPLISHMENT."

JAMES ALLEN

THE POWER OF FOCUS

Have you ever watched a child playing completely content with a certain toy until it sees another child with a different toy? Children often want whatever they see and may drop one perfectly enjoyable plaything as new play options are discovered. We are a lot like children in this respect. We want so many things that we are not consistent or devoted to our ultimate desires.

In his book, *Law of Attraction*, Michael J. Losier explains that "the first step in making the Law of Attraction work *for* you is to be clear about what you want." [8] If our thoughts, like a small child's, are scattered and running rampant after every new sensation we stumble on, our effort to manifest anything will be hampered and hindered.

When Thomas Edison was asked how he achieved so many successes he responded: "It's very simple. You and I

[8] Losier, Michael J., *Law of Attraction*, p. 23.

each have eighteen hours a day. You spend those eighteen hours doing a number of unrelated things. I spend it doing just one thing." If we want to achieve anything through the Law of Attraction, we must learn to focus. We should get one specific desire in our mind and in our heart. It should flow through every aspect of our being. We need to forget the distractions, temptations and side-desires and move with full power toward the one thing we want most.

An old military strategy asserted: "Divide and conquer." Armies become weak when they are divided. So does the power of the subconscious mind. If our time and efforts are divided among too many desires, we will be unable to concentrate and manifest our biggest aspirations as easily as if we focus that concentration on one specific manifestation. Distractions always drive us away from the main purpose of our lives. As Ralph Waldo Emerson stated: "The one prudence in life is concentration; the one evil dissipation." In other words, it is wise to focus and foolish to overindulge.

In his book, *As a Man Thinketh*, James Allen counsels us to conceive of a "legitimate purpose" in our heart, "and set out to accomplish it." [9] A strong desire and a specific purpose imbue the Law of Attraction with greater power. "Thought allied fearlessly to purpose," continues Allen, "becomes creative force: he who knows this is ready to become something higher and stronger than a mere bundle of wavering thoughts and fluctuating sensations; he who does this has become the conscious and intelligent wielder of his

---

[9] Allen, James, *As a Man Thinketh*, p. 45.

mental powers." [10]

This is a natural principle. "Where your treasure is," taught Matthew in the New Testament, "there will your heart be also." [11]

It is fine to have multiple desires. It's okay to have a vision board plastered with all we'd love to accomplish in our lifetime. But our focus cannot be on everything at once. We should limit that focus to a few major desires, and as we accomplish those, we can then begin adding the others.

To achieve any positive result through the Law of Attraction, we must have our hearts set on our greatest desire. We will always produce a result. We need to assure ourselves that it is the result we are hoping for by focusing particularly on that one desire.

You've probably heard the expression, "jack of all trades," but remember that a jack of all trades is a master of none. If we are trying to manifest several different things at the same time, we will send our subconscious thoughts scattering in every direction. If we focus all our thoughts and efforts on one desire, our subconscious will seek out that desire with laser-like pinpoint accuracy.

Michael J. Losier explains that "you attract to your life whatever you give your attention, energy, and focus to, whether wanted or unwanted." [12] We should concentrate on

---

[10] Ibid, p. 49.
[11] Matthew 6:21.

our power to create. In *The Power of Attraction*, I wrote that "focus and concentrated thought are the true method for reaching, awakening and manifesting the wonderful potential power of the world within you." [13]

The power of wholehearted, one-directional focus can become the most valuable asset in our life. Remember, you get what you focus on, so focus on what you want.

[12] Losier, Michael J., *Law of Attraction*, p. 18.
[13] Claysen, Steven, *The Power of Attraction*, DeepEnd Books, p. 134.

Insight & Inspiration

*"MAN IS MADE
OR UNMADE
BY HIMSELF."*

JAMES ALLEN

THE 'AS IF' PRINCIPLE

When it comes to the Law of Attraction, it really is the thought that counts. Our greatest strength lies in the creative powers of the mind. The mind is like a garden. We either cultivate useful, beautiful plants (thoughts) purposely or we allow negative, destructive plants to thrive there by default.

Harvard psychologist, William James, developed what he has called the 'as if' principle. The 'as if' principle states that if we wish to possess something, an emotion, a qualification, a lifestyle, etc., we should act 'as if' we already had it. We should let it get a hold on us. We need to let it possess us. We must infuse our minds with the thought that we already have it. As Shakespeare said: "Assume a virtue if you have it not." No one has ever determined just how far the mind can go in shaping our circumstances.

Every thought we think has an impact on our personality and, consequently, on our success or failure at achieving the things we desire. When we express these thoughts in words, we significantly increase the force and power of our thinking. We are, ultimately, what we believe and feel. King Solomon wrote that we are what we think in our hearts. People can make themselves sick simply by thinking that they are sick. Wouldn't it also be true that we could make ourselves healthy by thinking healthy thoughts, or wealthy by thinking prosperous thoughts, or confident by thinking confidently about ourselves?

The British Army once tested the power of thinking on three individuals. They selected three men to determine the power of mental attitude on physical performance. The strength of these men was tested using a simple gripping device. Under normal circumstances, the three men had a gripping strength of about 100 pounds. When a scientist put them under hypnosis and made them believe that they were very weak, their best effort only registered an average of 39 pounds. Still under hypnosis, the scientist told the three men that they were extraordinarily strong. Their average grip rose to 142 pounds. When these men believed in themselves, their strength increased by nearly 300% over when they thought they were weak.

James Allen tells us that we hold "the key to every situation" and we contain the "transforming and re-generative agency" by which we make ourselves into whatever we desire. [14] It is significantly important what and how we think! The power of suggestion is tremendous.

---

[14] See Allen, James, As a Man Thinketh, p. 14.

To gain anything in life, we should cultivate and think and act the things we would like to be. When we have the energy to choose our own fate, we can obtain any desire we have in life if we pursue it. Arthur Simons wrote that "there is no dream that may not come true."

In *The Lehrman Project,* I wrote of a concept known as Tabula Rasa. In that particular section of the book, I mention that "when you believe something to be true, it becomes true for you, no matter what the facts may indicate to the contrary. Everything we are today is the result of an idea or an impression we took in and accepted as true. When we change the way we think and feel about ourselves and our world, then the world around us changes." [15]

The largest ocean cannot sink even the smallest ship unless the water gets inside it. Allowing negative thinking into our mind is no different than poisoning our own drinking water. It is destructive and dangerous. When weak, negative, destroying thoughts get into our insides, we are in trouble and sinking fast. It is mental suicide.

William James explains that "if you form a picture in your mind of what you would like to be, and you keep and hold that picture there long enough, you will soon become exactly as you have been thinking."

The best road to success in any endeavor is to dream big, think big and give substance to your thoughts by acting

---

[15] Claysen, Steven, *The Lehrman Project,*

big, by acting 'as if'. When our actions and attitudes reflect our passions and desires, we saturate ourselves with the power of attraction and then nothing can be withheld from us.

This is the 'as if' principle.

INSIGHT & INSPIRATION

*"GRATITUDE IN
ADVANCE IS THE
MOST POWERFUL
CREATIVE FORCE IN
THE UNIVERSE."*

NEALE DONALD WALSH

THE POWER OF GRATITUDE

Our potential is infinite. Throughout all of nature, abundance is the governing concept. Our universe contains billions of galaxies. Our galaxy contains billions of stars and planets. Lack and limitation are non-existent. In nature, the natural flow is toward abundance.

The old saying that "you can count the seeds in an apple, but you can't count the apples in a seed" is a powerful truth. One seed sprouts and blossoms and then creates many more seeds which, in turn, all create more seeds.

Our thoughts are like seeds, sprouting and blossoming into the circumstances and situations that make up our lives. In other words, our method of thinking, our personal thought patterns, create our world.

Gratitude is a thought pattern that is forcefully bound to our emotions. Like a tiny seed, gratitude will take root and eventually blossom into the events, environments and occurrences that make up our daily lives. The fruits of gratitude are opportunity and abundance.

Being grateful in advance is one of the greatest tricks played on the mind. Being grateful for something that we don't actually have yet stimulates the subconscious brain and activates the Law of Attraction to create the condition we are already grateful for. As Paulina Vargas suggests: "My grateful heart is a magnet that attracts everything I desire." A grateful heart is a magnet for miracles.

Our consciousness creates our world. In the book, *The Power of Attraction*, I wrote: "To produce results, thought must be permeated with desire. Desire is a form of love and love imparts vitality to thought and enables it to grow." [16]

Gratitude is one of the deepest expressions of love and there is always something to be grateful for. Marc Reklau wrote of a study on gratitude conducted by Robert Emmons and Michael McCullough at the University of California Davis. Participants were asked to write down every night five things for which they were grateful. Emmons and McCullough discovered that the participants who created their gratitude lists were more optimistic, happier, healthier, more generous, more benevolent, and much more likely to achieve their goals than participants who didn't have a

---

[16] Claysen, Steven, *The Power of Attraction*, p. 95.

gratitude list.

Mr. Reklau writes that "gratitude recharges you with energy, boosts your self-worth, and is directly linked to physical and mental well-being. It leads you directly to happiness." [17] Science has discovered that we can re-wire our brains for happiness by simply thinking of three things we are grateful for every day for twenty-one days.

What if our life is not going so well and we are struggling to feel happy or grateful for anything? (Believe me, I've been there!) Keep in mind that all the events, circumstances, and conditions we undergo were essential to bringing us to where we are today. Therefore, if we are grateful for anything, we should be grateful for everything. The most powerful weapon against our daily struggles is to be grateful anyway.

Everything we receive in life comes through the Law of Attraction. If we express gratitude for what we don't have but desire to have, we are projecting a powerful thought that will initiate the realization of our desire. Time means nothing to the subconscious mind. It only comprehends the present moment. When we feel gratitude in the present for the things we desire in the future, we are opening the floodgates of manifestation.

Gratitude emits a certain psychodynamic energy. It empowers us to focus more on the positive and lures us away

---

[17] Reklau, Marc, *The Life-Changing Power of Gratitude.*

from the negative. This process generates positivity, confidence, and assurance. It also draws our attention away from harmful egocentricity and opens us up to becoming more. I believe it was Brian Tracy who said: "All that you appreciate, appreciates."

When we direct our focus and mental energy toward the beneficial aspects of our lives through gratitude, greater benefits are the sure result. To be filled with gratitude is one of the most important principles for manifesting our desires. When we receive *all* things with gratitude, we place ourselves in a position to receive even more.

Michael J. Losier explains in *Law of Attraction* that "appreciation and gratitude are the highest forms of vibration. When you're appreciating something, you're offering a feeling and vibration of pure joy…. Purposely taking time to treasure every day means that you are intentionally offering strong, pure positive vibrations." [18] Whenever we are thinking about or writing down our feelings of gratitude, we are offering a vibration and the Law of Attraction will reveal to us more of what we are vibrating.

A vital principle in activating, energizing, and profiting from the Law of Attraction is to possess an active and constant attitude of gratitude.

---

[18] Losier, Michael J., *Law of Attraction*, p. 81.

INSIGHT & INSPIRATION

*"A PARTICULAR TRAIN OF
THOUGHT PERSISTED IN, BE IT
GOOD OR BAD, CANNOT FAIL
TO PRODUCE ITS RESULTS ON
THE CHARACTER AND
CIRCUMSTANCES. A MAN
CANNOT DIRECTLY CHOOSE
HIS CIRCUMSTANCES, BUT HE
CAN CHOOSE HIS THOUGHTS,
AND SO INDIRECTLY, YET
SURELY, SHAPE HIS
CIRCUMSTANCES."*

JAMES ALLEN

THE AFFIRMATION PRINCIPLE

We are constantly talking to ourselves. This self-talk, whether it is negative or positive, is a continuous on-going activity that fills our minds. I often ask clients: "If you spoke to a friend the same way you speak to yourself, how long would you have that friend?"

The subconscious mind cannot reason. It takes us at our word. If we constantly repeat expressions like:

"Nothing ever works out for me."
"I'm such a loser."
"Nobody could ever love me."
"I'm invisible to my friends."

...then we have expressed a condition and our subconscious mind will respond by creating that condition for us.

For some of us, our thoughts float like driftwood on the ocean, tossed about by the force of whatever waves are pounding the shoreline. For others, our thoughts are like high-speed bullet trains racing into our past and then running ahead into our future. In either case, these unrestrained thoughts are also creating and manifesting constantly.

This is why we must always pay attention to our self-talk. If our thoughts and internal dialogue are in harmony with our desires, then we will attract those desires into existence. If our talk is negative, limiting, or self-defeating in any way, then we will manifest the discordant and inharmonious conditions that correlate with our thinking.

We should pay attention to our self-talk and ensure that it is in harmony with our desires. If it isn't, we need to replace it with better thoughts and improved language.

We can best do this through affirmations. An affirmation is a declaration designed to reprogram our thinking by implanting the desired thought into our subconscious minds through repetition. It is a consciously chosen set of words that reflects our desires. Affirmations will replace undesirable and destructive thinking. They can redirect our random mental chatter and erase the old programming that runs like a looped tape through our thinking.

An effective affirmation can actually change who we are. We can use affirmations to create new ideas, a new self-image, improved thought patterns, a more effective belief system and anything else we desire. We can affirm anything we want.

Affirmations can be as simple as saying, *I am kind*. Repeating these words over and over will makes us kinder human beings faster and more effectively than if we constantly try to remember to do random acts of kindness. Once we change our belief and thinking, the actions will naturally follow.

Disciplined repetition of empowering affirmations will activate and energize supportive thoughts that will soon become the basis for a new way of thinking, acting, and living.

Knowing that this is true, we might ask: "Then why doesn't every poor person just keep repeating: 'I am wealthy. I am wealthy. I am wealthy.'?" Why doesn't every overweight person simply repeat, 'I am slender, I am skinny, I am thin.'?" If it is really that simple, why doesn't everyone have everything they desire?

In *Law of Attraction*, Michael Losier explains that "the Law of Attraction does not respond to the words you use or the thoughts you think." [19]

I hear you now... "Wait a minute," you're saying, "didn't you just say that if our thoughts and dialogue are in harmony with our desires, we will attract those desires into existence?" Yes, I did but please let me finish Mr. Losier's

---

[19] Losier, Michael J., *Law of Attraction*, p. 50.

statement.

"The Law of Attraction does not respond to the words you use or the thoughts you think. *It simply responds to how you feel about what you say and how you feel about what you think.*"

The Law of Attraction responds to energy, to vibration. The higher our vibration, the greater our likelihood of manifesting our desires. Each time we repeat an affirmation, we have a reaction based completely on the feelings these words or thoughts stir in us. Someone who is overweight, for example, can stand in front of the mirror saying, "I am thin" all day and nothing may ever change because they are simultaneously feeling "I am so fat!" Their feelings are creating negativity. The vibrations they send out are damaging.

When we emit a vibration, any vibration, the Law of Attraction responds by giving us more. The negative vibration of self-loathing, of doubt and disbelief, will bring us more of what we don't want.

If we say, "I'd like to own a home," the Law of Attraction begins orchestrating the events that will bring us a home. At the same time, we create a self-sabotage situation by wondering how we will ever be able to afford a home in this market. Our feelings of fear and doubt are canceling our positive desire for a home and replacing it with the negative energy that will keep us living with mom and dad the rest of our lives.

Michael Losier offers the solution of creating a Desire Statement as your affirmation. "A Desire Statement is an effective tool for raising your vibration...A Desire Statement is a much more effective tool for keeping your desire at the center of your attention and raising your vibration." [20] A Desire Statement could begin with:

"I am in the process of..."
"I've decided to..."
"I love knowing that..."
"I'm excited to be..."
For example:
I love knowing that I am achieving my ideal weight.
Or, I'm excited to be purchasing my own home.
Or, I am in the process of attracting all that I desire.

A fundamental principle of the Law of Attraction is that feeling imparts vitality to thought. Any thought infused with positive feelings becomes an unstoppable creative force. If we want more out of life, we must affirm more.

---

[20] Losier, Michael J., *Law of Attraction*, p. 49, 51.

INSIGHT & INSPIRATION

"THEY WHO HAVE NO CENTRAL PURPOSE IN THEIR LIFE FALL AN EASY PREY TO PETTY WORRIES, FEARS, TROUBLES, AND SELF-PITYING'S."

JAMES ALLEN

THE POWER OF OBJECTIVES

Being successful at manifesting our desires through the Law of Attraction requires that we have an objective; a clear path about where we want to go, how we are going to get there, and what we are going to do once we arrive. Successful manifestation becomes so much easier with an objective that is clearly visualized and deeply desired.

Think of the pull of a small magnet. The force of its attraction increases the closer the magnet comes to the object it is attracting. This is also true in manifesting our desires through the Law of Attraction. Unless we give the object of our desire special attention, it will seem unimportant to the subconscious mind. We need an objective, something that our subconscious can tie into.

I read once that "genius is the power to visualize the objective." To properly visualize our desire, it must be clearly defined and cemented into our subconscious mind. Our desire should become a focal point, like a star we steer our ship by. If we are constantly changing our objective, we will truly make little progress.

As I explain in *The Power of Attraction*: "There is a vast difference between simply thinking and actually directing your thoughts consciously, systematically, and constructively. Thought is creative and will automatically correlate with the object of your thinking and bring it into manifestation."

The principal element to the law of objectives is to learn to "pre-live" our desire. In other words, we determine exactly what it is we want to manifest, we write that objective down daily, and then we allow our minds to move into the future and live that desire as though it were present. How?

Mentally catalogue all the pleasure you will experience when your desire is granted or fulfilled.

Think of how proud your family or friends will be when they see what you have accomplished.

Think of the accolades you will receive for your achievement.

Magnify the importance of each future accomplishment, achievement and desire obtained.

One of the paramount differences between successful manifestation and failure to manifest is that successful people focus on the future objective whereas unsuccessful people focus on the present and see nothing significant or spectacular in the future. The temporary let-downs of the present will not stop someone whose vision and focus are held in the future.

I love hiking the Rocky Mountains but if I were to focus on every footstep it takes me to reach the summit, I would easily become discouraged and quit. When I keep my mind focused on the magnificent vista and panoramic view from the top, then I climb with pleasure.

Consider this: Until 1926 no woman had ever successfully swum across the English Channel. An automobile company offered a brand-new Buick convertible and $2500 in cash to the first woman who could accomplish this feat. A 19-year-old American girl by the name of Gertrude Ederle wanted that automobile so badly that she determined to swim the English Channel. Part way across Gertrude's strength gave out. She couldn't go on. As she floated in the channel waiting to be taken out of the water, she closed her eyes and envisioned that beautiful Buick convertible. Visualizing the object of her desire gave her a surge of strength and she again began swimming. She did not stop until her feet reached the opposite shore. Gertrude Ederle became the first woman to swim the English Channel because she held a close image of her future objective.

All our passions and desires are located in the subconscious mind. They are a part of the imagination. If we keep our imagination focused on the objective, we have power. If we concentrate on the obstacle, we have discouragement.

Napoleon once stated: "I see only the objective. The obstacle must give way." Napoleon won his battles in his head before he ever won them on the battlefield. He saw the objective and everything else he ignored. We should practice in our own imaginations this same one-directional concentration with a clearly defined objective.

The imagination is an incredible tool. Allow it to run ahead, to step into the future to define what lies ahead. Don't rely solely on your own perspective because it can be tricked and deceived when robbed of the panorama of what awaits in the future. Let your subconscious live with the object of your desire; make it as enticing as possible; light it up like a beacon on the seashore. Raise the image of your objective to a heroic size!

Gradually the subconscious magnet of the Law of Attraction will become stronger and stronger until the complete manifestation of your desire cannot be withheld from you.

INSIGHT & INSPIRATION

"YOU HAVE THE FREEDOM TO MAKE YOUR OWN CHOICES. CHOOSE THOUGHTS OF HEALTH, HAPPINESS, PEACE AND ABUNDANCE AND YOU WILL REAP FABULOUS DIVIDENDS IN ALL YOUR RELATIONSHIPS."

JOSEPH MURPHY

THE BOOMERANG PRINCIPLE

Would you like to attract tremendous personal power?

Would you like to be trusted, respected, and loved?

Would you like people to treat you better?

The good news is all of this can be yours! The answer to obtaining these qualities as well as many others is the powerful gem of the boomerang principle.

An aboriginal boy from the bush country of Australia said to his father, "I'd like to get a new boomerang, but I can't get rid of the one I already have."

The boomerang principle states that whatever we throw out to life, we receive in return. The greatest teacher who ever lived, and the greatest expert in human relations, made this statement: "Do to others what you would have them do to you." This is a principle we can rely on. It is one of the most powerful combination of words in the human language. It was taught centuries before Jesus actually articulated those powerful words. Confucius, Zoroaster, and Mohammed all proclaimed the same idea. It has been practiced by the most successful people on the planet and yet, to most of the human population, this principle remains a largely unused and underappreciated mystery.

We are human magnets. Our actions, attributes and even our inner and secret thoughts attract in kind. James Allen reveals that people "imagine that thought can be kept secret, but it cannot; it rapidly crystallizes into habit, and habit solidifies into circumstance." [21] Like begets like. When we categorically comprehend the principle of action and reaction, we can stimulate any desired response in others. If we want smiles, we give smiles. If we want others to like us, we first like them. If we want to speak poorly of someone behind their back, we can expect a magnified retaliation in response.

Joseph Murphy explains in *The Power of Your Subconscious Mind* that "the thought you have about the other person is *your* thought, because *you* are thinking it. Your thoughts are creative. Therefore, you actually create in your own experience what you think and feel about the other person. The suggestion you give to another, you give to yourself as well, because your mind is the creative medium." [22]

Applying the boomerang principle is essential to changing your thinking and changing your life. In *The*

[21] Allen, James, *As a Man Thinketh*, pg. 34.
[22] Murphy, Joseph, *The Power of Your Subconscious Mind*, p. 204.

Lehrman Project I explain that creating powerful changes "requires expanding your ideas and imagination about the person you are and the person you would like to become. It is about rising above your current situation, with its limitations and problems, and seeing yourself living the life you desire. This type of thinking requires practice.

"In developing effective relationships with a spouse, a co-worker, your children, or anyone else for that matter, your commission is to monitor, manage and control your thinking. One of the paramount qualifications you can acquire in this life is the ability to effectively communicate, negotiate, influence, and persuade other people. This ability is characterized by an elevated compassion, sensitivity and awareness of the thoughts, feelings, motivations, and desires of the people around you...

"Keep your words and thoughts clearly and completely focused on the type of relationship you really want. At the same time, you must refuse to think about what you don't want. Your primary intention should always be to make positive subconscious communication a habitual way of thinking."

The boomerang principle has possibilities in both good and bad. In fact, this powerful principle has sometimes been referred to as the law of retaliation. It involves the ancient philosophy of "an eye for an eye and a tooth for a tooth," except the response is usually magnified and multiplied considerably. For instance, if one nation attacks another, the attacked nation will usually respond with increased force and destruction. This concept works on individuals as well. If I insult you to your face, you will likely throw a bigger insult to mine. But if I am gracious toward you, you will most likely be gracious in return. When we apply force and push others around, we will receive evil for evil, gossip for gossip, animosity for animosity multiplied and increased.

When we do good to those who wish to harm us, we disarm, and we dominate. As Lincoln said: "Do I not destroy my enemies when I make them my friends?"

Joseph Murphy recommends the following process for creating and maintaining a harmonious balance in your relationships with others. [23]

- As you would want people to think about you, think you about them in like manner.
- As you would want people to feel about you, feel you about them in like manner.
- As you would want people to act toward you, act you toward them in like manner.

The Boomerang Principle contains a power that is too strong for people to resist. It conquers every resistance it encounters. When we learn how to use it effectively, it will change our lives for the better. Try this formula for thirty days. Send kindness out into the world and watch it boomerang right back to you!

---

[23] Murphy, Joseph, *The Power of Your Subconscious Mind*, pp. 203, 204.

Insight & Inspiration

*"HE WHO HAS
CONQUERED DOUBT
AND FEAR HAS
CONQUERED FAILURE.
HIS EVERY THOUGHT IS
ALLIED WITH POWER,
AND ALL DIFFICULTIES
ARE BRAVELY MET AND
WISELY OVERCOME."*

JAMES ALLEN

THE POWER OF CONFIDENCE

I hear it from students. I hear it from clients. I see it constantly on social media. "I've been trying to manifest *blank* but it just doesn't work for me." The real question is: "What's holding me back? Why isn't the Law of Attraction working for me?"

I have discovered that confidence is needed in every aspect of our lives. Think of how many plans and desires go unanswered due to a lack of confidence in our dreams, in our goals, in our simplest desires. Thousands go to their graves never having reached their full potential simply because they lacked confidence. One of the most important qualities we can develop in using the Law of Attraction is confidence.

We need to have confidence in our ability to manifest our desires (self-confidence) as well as confidence that the Law of Attraction will absolutely give to us the very thing we desire. I remember my first attempt at using the Law of Attraction. I was a little skeptical. I was very unsure of myself and my abilities. I felt awkward. But a skilled teacher had told me: "You don't have to be an absolute believer to get results. You just have to entertain the possibility that you could get results." The results I achieved on my first attempt were so evident and obvious that I soon became "an absolute believer."

It is easily apparent that confidence is key to using the Law of Attraction to manifest our ultimate dreams and desires. In *The Lehrman Project: Experiments in Subconscious Communication,* I quote motivational speaker Brian Tracey who said: "Whatever you expect, with confidence, becomes your own self-fulfilling prophecy." Fortunately, confidence is a trait that anyone can develop. I'd like to offer 5 simple steps to developing confidence that can help anyone learning to use the Law of Attraction.

1. The best way to develop confidence is to practice being confident every day. As we read in a previous chapter, if we wish to possess something, an emotion, a qualification, a lifestyle, etc., we should act 'as if' we already had it. If we can practice having confidence in the little things, we will soon have the confidence to manifest anything we truly desire.

2. Another excellent way to develop confidence is to fill our minds with confidence. We can think about confidence. We should read about confidence. We can envision ourselves acting with confidence. We can think of confident people whom we admire. Our thoughts are like a bright, rich dye and our minds are colored by the thoughts we hold. As William James said: "If you form a picture in your mind of what you would like to be, and you keep and hold that picture there

long enough, you will soon become exactly as you have been thinking."

3. We can develop confidence by demonstrating to ourselves that we are already confident. Anyone can be confident for one day. And if we can be confident for one day, then why not for one week? Or for one month? If we can be confident for one month, why can't we be confident all year? We can look at those areas of our lives where we use our initiative, our personal resourcefulness, where we carry out our plans or stand up for ourselves. We can and should recognize when and where we are feeling, acting and being confident, and these moments will soon stand out in our lives.

4. We must remember that fear can be blinding, even fear of failure. We should remove all doubts and negative thinking from our minds. "Our doubts are traitors," wrote Shakespeare, "and make us lose the gift we oft might win, by failing to attempt."

5. Finally, we should follow through with our desires, dreams, goals, and convictions. It is easy to quit. It is easy to be thrown off track. When we question and doubt our abilities, our confidence wanes and withers. We don't need to know the process of how our desires will manifest. The *how* is not our concern. Wondering about how we will manifest our desires contains an element of doubt and a lack of confidence. We simply need to allow the Law of Attraction to work for us; we need to allow the Universe to bring our desires into reality.

The strongest factor for success in activating,

energizing, and profiting from the Law of Attraction is self-confidence; believing we can succeed, believing we deserve to succeed, believing we will succeed. It takes time to develop confidence, but it is certainly worth it. We learn by doing and if we can *act* confident in our abilities to manifest our desires today, we will find it even easier to be confident in the Law of Attraction tomorrow.

When that happens, we will no longer ask, "Why isn't this working for me?" We will, instead, become "an absolute believer."

INSIGHT & INSPIRATION

"GOOD THOUGHTS AND ACTIONS CAN NEVER PRODUCE BAD RESULTS; BAD THOUGHTS AND ACTIONS CAN NEVER PRODUCE GOOD RESULTS. THIS IS BUT SAYING THAT NOTHING CAN COME FROM CORN BUT CORN, NOTHING FROM NETTLES BUT NETTLES. MEN UNDERSTAND THIS LAW IN THE NATURAL WORLD, AND WORK WITH IT; BUT FEW UNDERSTAND IT IN THE MENTAL AND MORAL WORLD (THOUGH ITS OPERATION THERE IS JUST AS SIMPLE AND UNDEVIATING), AND THEY, THEREFORE, DO NOT COOPERATE WITH IT."

JAMES ALLEN

THE SEED PRINCIPLE

If we place a seed in the ground, it will slowly and imperceptibly begin to germinate. Eventually that seed will produce an abundant harvest. Beneficial seeds will always produce beneficial harvests. Harmful seeds will always produce harmful harvests.

We all have deeply hidden thoughts and feelings buried like seeds in the subconscious soil beneath our conscious awareness. Some of these seeds are beneficial and produce good fruit but some of them may be harmful and destructive, producing harmful and destructive events in our lives. Our outer world will always mirror the inner world of these subconscious thoughts and feelings.

In *As a Man Thinketh*, James Allen explains that our minds "may be likened to a garden, which may be intelligently cultivated or allowed to run wild; but whether cultivated or neglected, it must and will, bring forth. If no useful seeds are put into it, then an abundance of useless weed seeds will fall therein and will continue to produce their kind." [24]

We have a garden full of buried seeds; quotes, comments, and thoughts about ourselves, about our circumstances, about our abilities, about our finances. These seeds have been planted by our parents, our teachers, and our colleagues. What we experience in our day-to-day living is the harvest from those buried seeds. They confirm, validate, and re-enforce the hidden thoughts and beliefs of our subconscious minds.

James Allen reminds us that "just as a gardener cultivates his plot, keeping it free from weeds, and growing the flowers and fruits which he requires, so shall a man tend the garden of his mind, weeding out all the wrong, useless, and impure thoughts, and cultivating toward perfection the flowers and fruits of right, useful, and pure thoughts." [25]

As I explain in *The Lehrman Project*, if we want to change our circumstances (whatever they may be), we need to reprogram our subconscious thinking—replacing inaccurate, negative thoughts and feelings with the positive thoughts and feelings that will bring us the results we are seeking.

Concerning our finances, Fredric Lehrman suggests: "Look at your thoughts about money and start changing your thoughts. The money will then respond differently." This is

---

[24] Allen, James, *As a Man Thinketh*, p. 17.
[25] Ibid.

true in any circumstance, situation, or condition in life. If we look at our thoughts about our relationships and start changing those thought, our relationships will change. If we look at our thoughts about our careers, our lifestyles, our health, and we change those thoughts, then those conditions will also begin to change.

Making a list of our most negative thoughts will help us bring these deep-seated thoughts and feelings to the surface so we can view them and choose a replacement thought and feeling.

Many years ago, after listening to Tony Robbins, I sat down with a note pad and created a list of my hidden thoughts about money. On the left side of the paper, I listed my negative thoughts about money and on the right, I wrote a new, positive belief that would reprogram my old thoughts and feelings about money. This process not only transformed my beliefs about money, but it also transformed my financial world as well.

We should remember that "every thought seed sown or allowed to fall into the mind, and to take root there, produces its own, blossoming sooner or later into act, and bearing its own fruitage of opportunity and circumstance. Good thoughts bear good fruit, bad thoughts bad fruit." [26]

It is a good practice to examine our own inner thoughts, feelings, and beliefs. Where did they come from?

---

[26] Allen, James, *As a Man Thinketh*, p. 21.

Are they our own thoughts or were they planted in our cerebral soil by someone else? Are they producing a beneficial harvest or a harmful harvest? In order to effectively activate, energize, and profit from the Law of Attraction, we should pay close attention to our own thoughts and beliefs and examine what is actually happening in our subconscious thinking. We can remove the negative "weed" seeds planted years ago and replace them with positive, fruitful, productive seeds that will provide a bountiful harvest of our positive desires.

Insight & Inspiration

"A MAN CAN ONLY RISE, CONQUER, AND ACHIEVE BY LIFTING UP HIS THOUGHTS. HE CAN ONLY REMAIN WEAK, AND ABJECT, AND MISERABLE BY REFUSING TO LIFT UP HIS THOUGHTS."

JAMES ALLEN

THE POWER OF MOTIVATION

The notion exists that behind every act lies a motive for that act. The science of crime detection intrinsically involves the concept of motive. In a criminal investigation, if a motive is discovered, the perpetrator can usually be identified. A well-trained and successful detective always looks for a motive. Crime detection is the power of motivation—*in reverse*. A detective, seeing the results of a crime, works backward to find the motive.

The Law of Attraction begins with a motive and works forward toward the result. The one word that possesses the power to activate and energize the Law of Attraction in manifesting our desires is motivation. People tend to dawdle and postpone. We forget or we lose interest in the things we want to achieve. We get discouraged or grow tired or lazy in our efforts to manifest our hearts' desires. Sometimes we just seem to have too many side interests which distract, deter, and throw us off track. Our idleness and apathy soon undermine our confidence and eventually we either lie down, sit down, or fall down and then give up.

The greatest drawback in activating, energizing, and profiting from the Law of Attractions is not in doing it wrong; but in not doing it at all. "Our greatest fear," wrote Sterling Sill, "should not be that life will someday come to an end, but rather that it will never really have a beginning. The ability to breathe the breath of life into our own machinery is one of the greatest abilities in the world."

The power of motivation is the breath of life, the inherent force within each of us, that disrupts our inertia. It rekindles the fire in our souls. Fire requires oxygen. Motivation is the oxygen essential for manifesting the imaginary into reality. Without motivation, the flight of imagination is rendered wingless. English Prime Minister Disraeli stated that "the secret of success is constancy of purpose."

Our concern becomes maintaining our motivation, our constancy of purpose, through the distractions, inertia, and apathy that creep into our existence. The old-fashioned wristwatches had to be continuously wound to tell time. Today's cell phones need their batteries constantly charged. We, too, must have a technique to keep our mainspring tight and to keep our batteries charged.

No two people are the same and we all respond differently to varying stimuli but we each must discover the gems that keep us motivated toward achieving our individual dreams. The method and solution may be unique to us but whatever affectively motivates us should be identified and acted upon. Following are six suggestions that may help us wind up our mainspring and keep our motivational batteries fully charged:

1. Purpose.

Psychology demonstrates that we want to replicate events that bring us pleasure and contentment. No fulfillment in life will ever be greater than the rewards of realizing our sincerest purpose. Robert Louis Stevenson once said: "I know what pleasure is for I have done good work." Striving to achieve a strong purpose is one of life's greatest motivators.

2. Clear Goals.

Much of success at anything is the ability to visualize the desired outcome. Without a distinct visual or a well-defined written goal fixed in our minds, not much would get accomplished. A large part of success lies hidden in our power to visualize the object of our desire. Clear goals with a definite daily, weekly, monthly, and yearly plan will keep our motivation strong.

2. Passion.

Vince Lombardi said that winning isn't a sometime thing; it is an all-time thing. The satisfaction that comes from winning gives us great motivational power. What greater stimulant exists than the feeling that we are succeeding at manifesting our greatest desires through the Law of Attraction? Our most important aim, aspiration and ambition must be to energize, achieve and manifest our innermost desires.

3. Determination.

Success just makes sense, doesn't it? Consider the wisdom and reasonableness of succeeding. Our personal survival, the welfare of our families, the houses we live in, the type of car we drive, our security and lifestyle at retirement— almost everything we own and much of who we are depends on our ability to succeed. Failing in life just doesn't make sense (or cents).

4. Substantiation.

No contest would be challenging without a scorekeeper. The scoreboard makes the game interesting and stimulating. Confirmation and verification confirm our success. There is no way to know when we are on schedule. Determine your objective, then keep a definite record to determine your progress. Stay motivated through daily progress check-ups. I check my book sales every day.

5. Gratification.

Emotion is intricately connected to motivation. Feelings significantly effect actions. Emotion injected into the heart and mind can be an excellent motivator. Ideas carry moods. We can change our mood by changing our ideas and imagination. Vision boards, books, movies, and the like can inspire enthusiasm, drive determination, and actuate accomplishment. We should study material that gives us empowered thoughts and ideas.

Motivation creates motion; it gets us moving in the right direction. Socrates said: "He who would move the world must first move himself." Motivation animates us to act. Anyone willing to act can energize, activate, and profit from the Law of Attraction. Our power is in our thoughts. We need to stay motivated to think those thoughts that will create the world we desire. The more we use the power within us, the more we will draw to us.

INSIGHT & INSPIRATION

*"A CHANGE OF DIET
WILL NOT HELP A MAN
WHO WILL NOT
CHANGE HIS
THOUGHTS."*

JAMES ALLEN

THE PRACTICE PRINCIPLE

We all know the adage "Practice makes perfect." Well, that axiom isn't categorically accurate. Practice doesn't, in fact, make perfect, practice makes permanent. If we continually practice doing something wrong, we will never become perfect at it. Only perfect practice makes perfect.

If a child practices throwing a baseball incorrectly, he or she will never become a perfect pitcher. A champion golfer plays every stroke as though he were in an important tournament. Our subconscious minds are not aware of when we are simply practicing and when we are actually performing. Practice, discipline, and repetition, whether good or bad, positive or negative, makes us what we are.

When we think negative, belittling, or hurtful thoughts, the Universe assumes we are thinking in earnest and will grant us our wishes. We cannot allow ourselves to let down our guard, or to practice pretense in anything we do in life because we would be molding a deformity in our character and shifting away from the divine.

Jesus taught: "Love your enemies."

Why? Why should we *love* our enemies?

Because to practice hate is an extremely bad habit to get into.

If we practice loving our enemies, just imagine how good we will become at loving our friends! The subconscious cannot distinguish between genuine love and practicing love. To our minds, they are both the same.

Why are we taught to "return good for evil?"

For the same reason—we need the practice.

"The chain of habit," wrote Sterling Sill, "is too light to be felt until it is too strong to be broken."

Habit can be like certain diseases; in the beginning stages it may be easy to cure but difficult to recognize or diagnose. After time the disease becomes easy to recognize but difficult to cure. Every minute of every day we are practicing. We practice how we walk, how we think, how we feel, how we respond. The essential element to manifesting our deepest desires is to practice only the thoughts, feelings and actions that will improve us.

Our attitude, our thoughts, even our posture becomes habitual—the mental as well as the physical, the positive as well as the negative, the malignant as well as the beneficial.

We become worriers by worrying; we become doers by doing. We become positive thinkers by thinking positive thoughts and we become negative thinkers by thinking negatively.

After I experienced a back injury, my wife noticed that I was walking differently. Without realizing it I had changed the way I stepped to avoid feeling pain. After my back had healed, I continued, unaware, to walk as I had when I was in pain. It became an exceedingly difficult experience for me to retrain my body to walk normally.

When we are alone, we may tend to let our guard down. No one is watching and we can get away without thinking our best thoughts, feeling positive emotions, or performing constructively. This is backward progress. Through negligence we may quickly lose what took many painstaking years to accomplish. We slowly gather such a heavy weight of hurtful, harmful habits and our negativity becomes too unmanageable for our positive thoughts or feelings to control.

We should practice directing, guiding, and adjusting our thinking, our health, our habits, our feelings and never permit the practice of negative behaviors, thoughts, or emotions. Successfully manifesting positive circumstances and outcomes is determined by what we practice in and out of season. We can't perform positivity on stage if we practice negativity off stage. The human mind is a recording device that is always on.

Practice is a powerful tool for activating, energizing, and profiting from the Law of Attraction. It is exciting to contemplate the benefits this one remarkable gem can bring into our lives.

INSIGHT & INSPIRATION

"ALL THAT A MAN ACHIEVES AND ALL THAT HE FAILS TO ACHIEVE IS THE DIRECT RESULT OF HIS OWN THOUGHTS."

JAMES ALLEN

THE POWER OF WORDS

An unfortunate woman trudged through the deserted streets of Paris on a grey autumn morning. Starvation filled her face and belly; despair darkened her vacant eyes. With mechanical movements she tapped her drum while repeatedly vocalizing the word, bread..., bread..., bread. Her words initiated the French Revolution of 1789.

A painter works with color, the sculpture with shape, and the musician with tone. Color, form, and tone are beautiful and meaningful by virtue of their creative expression, but they fade into insignificance when compared with the power of speech. Poets and prophets use words to influence our feelings. Lawyers win cases, ministers save souls, statesmen make history, and salespersons convince us to buy all through the effective use of words. As stated in the song lyrics by The Police:

"Poets, priests, and politicians
Have words to thank for their positions."

Words are our most important tools, and one of the most effective means for activating, energizing, and profiting from the Law of Attraction.

Words are everywhere. We speak them, read them, write them, think them, see them, type them, and hear them in our heads. All words carry a vibration for the person who says or thinks them. The most significant and influential words you will ever speak are the words you say to yourself.

According to Michael J. Lozier, "Words are the common denominator for all steps in the attraction process." [27] The quality of the idea and the effectiveness of its expression determine what will happen within our minds and within our lives. Facts may constitute the material out of which claims are made, but passions, prejudices, sentiments, and personal emotions play a strong part in determining our actions and reactions to those facts. Action and reaction are activated, energized, and brought to life through the effective expression of words.

The power of words can do more than can ever be done by conquering weapons. We are all familiar with the adage, "The pen is mightier than the sword." As we become more aware of our use of language and its importance in our vibration, we will begin to notice whenever we make a

---

[27] Lozier, Michael J., *Law of Attraction*, p. 16.

negative statement.

The subconscious mind filters out certain words like no, not and don't. Whenever we use these words, we are actually internalizing in our minds the very idea that we are attempting to avoid. For example, if I said, do not think of an elephant, I guarantee that you would start thinking of an elephant almost immediately. Even though the instruction was to not do something, your subconscious edited out the negative part of that instruction. Many of our common expressions give more attention and energy to the negative. 'Don't get mad.' 'Don't worry.' 'Don't panic.' 'Don't look now.' 'Don't forget.' 'Don't be late.' When you hear a negative suggestion such as these, turn the negative into a positive by restating what you have just said. Instead of saying: "I can't be late for my appointment," try saying: "I always arrive on time."

The primary concern of speech is to address our affections, our passions, our prejudices, and our thoughts and feelings. Power resides in proper and appropriate use of language. Statesman have achieved greatness by the power and effectiveness of their speech. They dominate and lead the will of their followers by the power of words. To help us activate, energize, and profit from the Law of Attraction we need to rethink our thoughts and make them serve our purpose. As we reshape our words and thoughts, we will receive increased ability and power. Our words, powerfully spoken, will influence our ability to attract whatever we desire. The Universe will listen and follow our directions.

We can attract more and do so more effectively as we develop our ability to effectively use words to influence the Universe. As Sterling Sill taught: "Words, effectively used, are the magic carpet on which we fly to success."

INSIGHT & INSPIRATION

"VISUALIZATION IS SO POWERFUL THAT WHEN YOU KNOW WHAT YOU WANT, YOU WILL GET IT."

AUDRY FLACK

THE VISUALIZATION PRINCIPLE

Visualization is the process of creating mental images. To be able to manifest anything in our lives, we must first be able to visualize it. The world we create around us stems from the ideal that we hold in our subconscious minds. Therefore, the saying, "What you see is what you get," becomes true for all of us.

The process that leads to manifesting our desires begins with visualization. Joseph Murphy indicates that "the easiest and most obvious way to formulate an idea is to visualize it, to see it in your mind's eye as vividly as if it were alive... What you form in your imagination is as real as any part of your body. The idea and the thought are real and will one day appear in your objective world." [28]

The Universe is a constant act of creative visualization. We each possess this same creative power. If we can visualize

---

[28] Murphy, Joseph, *The Power of Your Subconscious Mind*, pp. 82, 83.

something as real, then it is real. Everything else involved in the manifestation process is merely technique, habit, and application.

We can illuminate our future with the light of visualization.

What do you see when you look down the path toward your future?

Nothing actually exists down that path except what you see ahead of you.

And everything that you see ahead of you is a conscious choice that you are making at this very moment.

We create every detail, every event, and every circumstance of our future through our present application of visualization. What you see really is what you get.

We need to see clearly where we are headed. We do this through visualization. Quoting the Book of Proverbs again: "Where there is no vision, the people perish." [29] If we have no vision for the direction our lives are headed, we will end up stumbling around in the dark. If we wish to control our future, we should consciously envision exactly what we want to create and manifest.

---

[29] Proverbs 29:18.

Imagination is an essential component in visualization. Through experience, knowledge, and good judgment, we can learn to trust our imaginations until we manifest the actual circumstance. Hope and fear, pleasure and pain are all created by our ability to visualize. The vision of our future is enhanced by our hopes, our determination and by the positiveness with which we see the attainment of our desires.

We shouldn't wait for random events to occur and then accept them as our fate. When we focus too much on the present, we tend to blot out the future. The vision we hold of our future life should be bright, pleasant and in complete harmony with our desires.

How hard is it to visualize receiving one dollar from the Universe? We could easily see ourselves finding a dollar bill in the gutter or in the pocket of a pair of pants we haven't worn for a long time. To the Law of Attraction, size has no meaning. If, through the Law of Attraction, we can manifest a dollar bill, then why not a ten-dollar bill? For the Law of Attraction, it is the same. No difference exists between one dollar and ten dollars.

Can you readily accept that fact? Bob Doyle stated that: "Size is nothing to the Universe. It is no more difficult to attract, on a scientific level, something that we consider huge to something that we consider infinitesimally small... It's all about what's going on in your mind." [30]

---

[30] Doyle, Bob, *The Secret*, p. 63.

When we understand this, when we can accept that whatever we ask of the Law of Attraction we can manifest into reality, then one dollar, or ten, becomes the same. And if one and ten are the same, then so are one and one thousand. And so are one and one million. The process is the same. The only limitation placed on our ability to manifest is the limitation we place on our method of thinking.

Effective visualization may take practice but with practice we can become proficient at creating a clear and beautiful pattern for our future. I suggest starting simple to build self-confidence and trust in the process. Practice visualizing things that already exist. Visualize your favorite food, or a flower or the face of a friend. Visualize your favorite color. Attract a tasty dessert or the perfect parking spot in front of the bank. Starting small is an easy way to experience the Law of Attraction. As we begin to expect great things, we will create our desired life in advance.

Through effective visualization we can construct our future, our new life, all within the confines of our imagination. Afterall, it will have to be built there before it will appear anywhere else.

Insight & Inspiration

"THE SOUL ATTRACTS
THAT WHICH IT
SECRETLY HARBORS;
THAT WHICH IT LOVES,
AND ALSO THAT WHICH
IT FEARS."

JAMES ALLEN

THE POWER OF FEAR

In his first inauguration speech, Franklin D. Roosevelt made the well-known statement: "We have nothing to fear but fear itself." His speech was charged with the rhetoric of hope and courage. Many see fear as detrimental to progress. They see it as an obstacle that troubles the soul and holds us back. People who accept this reality are often injured by it because nothing could be farther from the truth.

The capacity to fear was put into our nature to strengthen our courage, protect us from harm, and increase our capability for accomplishment. Shakespeare said: "To fear the worst, oft cures the worst." It is a perversion of our personalities to let fear inspire timidity, paralysis, dread, dismay, hysteria, or panic.

Fear is an important and constructive emotion. It is a force for good, provided we fear the right things at the right time. We ought to be afraid of some things, like bigotry and pettiness and dishonesty, but fear also keeps us on our feet and moving.

Unreasonable fear can make us blind and deaf (and sometimes dumb) but understood and controlled, fear can be a great ally. A child stays away from fire out of fear; people obey laws because of fear; we attend school out of fear of ignorance and unemployment. We work and save because we fear poverty and lack, we plan and think because we fear the result of misdirected effort. Wouldn't it make sense that we would want to stimulate rather than destroy these fears?

Fear of failure and weakness tends to make us stronger and safer. Fear is a warning flag. It prompts us to stop, look, and listen. It keeps us sharp and on our toes. The world would be a chaotic mess without the great and valuable controlling emotion of fear.

Fear can multiply our strength. In 2009, 185 lb. Nick Harris lifted a Mercury sedan to help a 6-year-old girl pinned beneath it. Also in 2009, Donna McNamee, Abigail Sicolo, and Anthony McNamee lifted a 1.1-ton Renault Clio off an 8-year-old boy. We can run faster or fight harder or do more work when we are fearful of something bad happening.

Like fire, fear is a valuable servant but a poor master. Let fear get out of control to a point where it becomes panic or hysteria and it causes great destruction. The road to activating, energizing, and profiting from the Law of Attraction is easily hampered by our unreasonable fears, but when motivated by a substantial, well controlled, well understood fear, our spiritual and mental muscles become strong. When we learn how to properly handle our fears, we become courageous in the achievement of our inner most desires.

We should not fear 'fear' but should recognize it and welcome it as an ally. In fact, the only place where it is possible to develop our resolution is in the presence of fear. Fear is the moving cause of most accomplishment. We should not try to avoid fear, but rather to appreciate, understand, and develop it. After all, don't most the things we fear or worry over correct themselves before they ever happen?

The most challenging test of human memory is to try to remember the things we worried about and fretted over and feared only ten years ago. Our greatest fears are usually those that never even materialized.

To activate, energize, and profit from the Law of Attraction, we should remember the counsel of Apollo: "Let not fear prevail above thy will."[31]

---

[31] From Eumenides by Aeschylus, 458 B.C. Translated by E. D. A. Morshead.

INSIGHT & INSPIRATION

"THE KEY TO ABUNDANCE IS MEETING LIMITED CIRCUMSTANCES WITH UNLIMITED THOUGHTS."

MARIANNE WILLIAMSON

THE ABUNDANCE PRINCIPLE

Think of the elaborate abundance with which Creation surrounds us. Anything and everything we might hope and wish for is easily within our reach. We are, without a doubt, intended to share in that abundance. There is more than enough to spare. Consider the richness of our natural resources. Think also of the resources in your own subconscious mind that lie buried and mostly unused.

Nature gives us everything in abundance and expects us to manifest that abundance in our lives. The Creator did not intend for us to be destitute or poverty-stricken. Consider this: Only one millionth part of the sun's rays reach our planet to maintain life; the rest of its beams dissipate in cold, empty space. Can you imagine that the Being who created such an abundant source of heat, light and energy intended for humanity to be deprived of the things we need for our happiness and sustenance? Do you believe that the Universe intended us to live in want, sickness, fear, ignorance, and insecurity?

Consider how abundantly nature rewards us for what we do. A single tomato seed can multiply itself a million times in one year. Ten forests can come from one acorn. If we plant one bushel of seed potatoes, we receive sixty bushels in return. One single potato carried to England by Sir Walter Raleigh in the sixteenth century multiplied itself into food for millions. A single apple seed can become a great tree, producing foliage, blossoms, fragrance, and fruit not just for one year, but for many lifetimes.

There are no signs of limitation in nature.

So why would we suffer limitation in any other area of our lives? Every ounce of energy we pour into our education can be returned to us fantastically multiplied. Every investment we make in the development of character, creativity, ingenuity, courage, and conscientiousness is also abundantly rewarded. Every determination we make in life returns to us many times over. Every manifestation of faith, even as tiny as a miniscule mustard seed, can move mountains.

Nature is rich and the Universe intends for us to be rich as well. The essence of the abundance principle is that we must believe in abundance. We must think abundance. We must expand our boundaries. We must increase our vision for greater accomplishments and let no thought of failure or limitation enter our conscious or subconscious minds. We can be more, do more and have more. Ralph Waldo Emerson rightly said that humanity "was intended to be rich."

There is no lack of opportunity. The Universe never intended for us to live as beggars. It never intended us to be poor or worried or unable to pay our bills when we are surrounded with abundance that is ours for the asking. "All things," said Jesus, "whatever you ask in prayer, believing, you shall receive." The important thing is to believe and take the first step. If we work toward our goals with all our hearts, why should the thought of failure even enter our heads?

When we think anxiety, disappointment, and failure, that is what we get. To utilize the abundance principle, we need to think strength, health, and prosperity. Our achievements today are the result of our past thoughts. Whatever value we place on our existence, life will give it to us.

As one poet wrote:

"I bargained with life for a penny,
Only to find dismayed,
That anything I had asked of life,
Life would have paid."

If we emphasize and visualize our worries, our fears, and our negative attitudes, we will eventually become saturated with them. We make our negative thoughts a reality by our habits of failure.

Many of us only see our limitations and we are defined by them. But consider that Napoleon and Caesar were epileptic and yet they became extremely powerful. Many people claiming welfare checks from the government are in better health than Julius Caesar when he was conquering the world. John Milton wrote *Paradise Lost*, one of the greatest pieces of literature, while he was totally blind and living in poverty. Abraham Lincoln had to borrow money for a train ticket to Washington, D.C. so he could give his inaugural address. Walt Whitman wrote: "Nothing external has any power over me."

We need to be careful about what we think because that is what we become. Thoughts are energy; thoughts are magnets that attract to us the various things we think. The greatest short cut to prosperity is to believe in it. "Give, and it shall be given to you; good measure, pressed down, and shaken together, and running over." [32] Nature is rich and it intends for all of us to have abundance in good measure, pressed down, shaken together, filled up and running over. All we need to do is follow the abundance principle.

---

[32] Luke 6:38.

INSIGHT & INSPIRATION

"TO AVOID CRITICISM, DO NOTHING, SAY NOTHING, BE NOTHING."

ELBURT HUBBARD

THE POWER OF CRITICISM

As a child, I always believed that the ostrich buries its head in the sand when it is frightened to hide from the danger that threatens it. As an adult, I discovered that ostriches do not do this. Someone has maligned the poor bird by assigning it human traits and characteristics. When an ostrich is frightened, it either fights or runs.

Think how this characteristic of trying to hide from our fears manifests itself in some people. When we are given a shot from a doctor or nurse, many of us close our eyes so we won't see ourselves get hurt. We turn away from the sight of blood or other unpleasant things. When we smell something unpleasant, we hold our noses. When we hear something unpleasant, we put our fingers in our ears. When life is too unpleasant, we take a tranquilizer.

Hiding from disagreeable facts is especially manifest when someone is trying to make suggestions to help us.

Criticism is one of the hardest medicines to take. This inability to learn the truth about ourselves is a stumbling block to activating, energizing, and profiting from the Law of Attraction.

Each of us should at least be aware of the tendency within us to hide from the facts, and those affected should develop the ability to look within themselves. Like a surgeon with a scalpel, cutting into living tissues, not to kill, but to examine and cure the body, we should practice the art of mental and emotional self-examination. Hiding from the facts about ourselves when those facts are unpleasant can hinder our ability to successfully manifest the desires of our hearts.

Advice is seldom valued, though there is a great deal of advising and exceedingly little listening. As a rule, we do not want advice; we want flattery. At some point, however, we must accept the truth about ourselves. Cato asserted that "the wise profit more from fools than fools do from the wise, for the wise will try to avoid the faults of fools, but fools seldom try to imitate the wise." We seldom scrutinize ourselves or our style of thinking to see whether our struggles in achieving our desires may be associated with our thought patterns.

The reason is obvious; we may not like what we are going to see but our judgment is no better than our information. When we deliberately shun criticism, our judgment becomes useless or harmful. Good or bad, almost the last thing anyone wants to hear is criticism and council.

Every one of us ought to have an employer or a partner or a counselor or a trusted friend who can, like a skilled surgeon, cut into the tissues of our attitudes and mental habits, not to kill but to cure.

If we are fortunate enough to have someone occasionally remind us of our thinking errors, we should listen, keeping our heads out of the sand and our eyes and ears open. If we really wish to manifest our hearts' desires, we need someone on the sidelines to coach and to observe and to warn.

INSIGHT & INSPIRATION

"THE ART OF KNOWING IS KNOWING WHAT TO IGNORE."

RUMI

THE FUSION PRINCIPLE

Did you ever find a fly in a bowl of soup? What was your reaction? One thing is certain: all the soup was spoiled.

I rented a room in a hostel for about 6 months. It was operated by a lovely German couple. Included in the cost of the room was breakfast and lunch. This wonderful German lady would serve warm cabbage soup before our lunch meal. We were required to eat the soup before we could have anything else. It was a bland and watery soup that consisted of nothing more than hot water, a few cabbage leaves, and some pepper for seasoning. After living with this couple for several weeks, I was slowly eating my soup when I noticed that what I thought was pepper seemed to have six little legs protruding out of its side. The pepper was, in reality, a small garden insect that fed on cabbage leaves.

If you put a drop of water in a bottle of ink, the ink is, for the most part, unchanged. But if you put a drop of ink into a glass of water, the entire glass is ruined. There is a saying that "the whole is judged by the part." This is known as the principle of fusion. The whole bowl of soup is considered spoiled, because of the small insect. The entire glass of water is ruined by the induction of a small drop of ink.

Often, we allow our negative thoughts and feelings to run together with our positive thinking. They fuse into one another. The nature of the whole takes on the character of the part. This creates the mental and emotional principle of fusion. It is like introducing a piece of moldy fruit into a bowl of fresh fruit; the moldy fruit will soon spoil the fresh fruit that is next to it.

Think of your personality qualities. Our personalities are the sum of our thoughts, feelings, and our spiritual nature. The thoughts we think, the character we develop by those thoughts, all constitute a part of our personality. We may have fifty positive character traits, but one negative element in our thinking can spoil the whole.

Are we being weigh down and held back in the pursuit of our desires by a negative personality millstone around our necks? The fusion principle will put in a cancellation order on all our positive desires. Whether we are moving toward our dreams or away from them, whether we are eliminating or acquiring negative mental and emotional deficiencies should be a matter of daily introspection and earnest concern. It will help us determine whether the principle of fusion is working for us or against us.

An important part of activating, energizing, and profiting from the Law of Attraction is removing the debris from our thoughts, feelings, and spiritual natures. A strong physical body has a well-regulated elimination system that regularly rids itself of waste and impurities. A vigorous and healthy mind operates on the same principle. Rid the mind of all negative debris because the fusion principle will fuse the negative with the positive. The whole is judged by the part, and the part is judged by the whole.

INSIGHT & INSPIRATION

"I HAVE CONSULTED WITH MY OWN GREAT SOUL."

HOMER

THE POWER OF INNER WEALTH

Abraham Lincoln was a child of nature, so close to the source of wisdom that he did not need to depend on books or educators, or schools; for his brain and heart had access to the timeless wisdom of the Universe.

A sense of divinity exists in all of us. A universal life seems, at times, to flow through us. The Hindus explain this marvelous human life with all its wonderful abilities by their belief in reincarnation. They attribute the things we do and know to an intelligence acquired in a previous incarnation.

The poet, Wordsworth says:

"Our birth is but a sleep and a forgetting:
The Soul that rises with us, our life's Star,
Hath had elsewhere its setting,
And cometh from afar:
Not in entire forgetfulness,

And not in utter nakedness,
But trailing clouds of glory do we come
From God, who is our home."

Some feel that at the time we are born we possess more knowledge than is found in all the books in all the libraries of the world. Instinct and emotion are not taught to us; they are instilled in us before birth. They spring out of nature when the time is right. We should never allow a lack of formal education to hold us back. Our minds are equipped to meet every need and we should learn to rely more on our own abilities and talents.

It is important that we understand that every human being has a great inner reservoir of unseen ability. We may summon this ability at any time to activate, energize, and profit from the Law of Attraction. We certainly should use these marvelous characteristics of ours more often.

Emerson believed that we become weak to the extent that we look outside ourselves for help. With the invention of the clock, people largely lost the power to tell time by the sun. When the mole stopped using its eyes, nature took away its eyesight. When we depend on outside information, confirmation, and validation, our innate power to manifest our desires is diminished.

However, when we unhesitatingly call upon the powers within us, *that* is when we learn our true strength and are able to work miracles of manifestation and realization. When we toss out all the false props we have been leaning on and lean instead on the power the Creator has placed within each of us, then we discover our true inner aptitude and ability.

The greatest area for exploration, discovery, and development is not in diamond mines or oil fields; nor is it the miracle of space exploration or the power of the internet. It is, instead, something that is buried very deep in the human personality. The whole field of intuition, instinct, revelation, or inspiration is relatively unexplored and still lies mostly beyond the furthermost limits of the imagination. Humanity still does not know its total capacity for initiative or accomplishment.

Imagine believing that inherent in every person there exists a sense of divinity. We all have a kinship with deity. A universal light and power flows through us. Imagine the incredible power to create and manifest that comes to us as a consequence. We each have a greater dignity than we suppose.

.

The greatest mistake that is ever made by human beings is that we under appraise the genius, the intelligence, and the tremendous possibility of ourselves.

Insight & Inspiration

"THERE IS COMPENSATION IN ALL THINGS."

ANNA LEONOWENS

THE KARMA OR COMPENSATION PRINCIPLE

Ralph Waldo Emerson pointed out that for every act there is an appropriate compensation. We cannot do any good thing without at some time, in some way, receiving a reward. Likewise, we cannot do a bad thing without suffering a damaging consequence.

The cause and the effect, the means and the end, the seed and the fruit cannot be separated from each other. The effect already blossoms in the cause, and the end always breeds in the means. The fruit is already hidden in the seed.

The karma principle is always observed in nature. Lightning is always followed by thunder. The cause-and-effect relationship is seen clearly between heavy rain and consequent flooding. Lack of rainfall leads to drought; excessive exposure to direct sunlight causes sunburn. The cause-and-effect relationship is present whenever one event could not have occurred without a preceding event.

Some may disagree with this principle, not recognizing its validity, because they have witnessed situations where compensation did not seem evident. Usually, the only problem is that these people were not patient enough.

If we want to be successful at manifesting our desires, if we want to activate, energize, and profit from the Law of Attraction, we must be willing to make the necessary investment. In life, you get back what you put in.

Our thoughts, behaviors, and actions create specific effects that manifest and create our life. This is our compensation. If we are not happy with the effects, we must simply change the causes that created them in the first place. The karma principle is, in fact, the cause that leads to the effects of the Law of Attraction.

The karma, or compensation, principle states that if we make the right decisions and take the right actions, we will undoubtedly achieve the success we envision for our lives — whether we are directly aware of it or not.

The compensation principle states that there are no accidents in this world. Everything that happens, whether good or bad, happens for a reason. The effects we create in our lives are a direct result of causes that come from within ourselves.

Because nothing happens by chance or luck, therefore everything happens for a reason as a direct result of the cause that we bring about from within.

Who we have been, who we are today, and whom we are becoming tomorrow, is, in essence, creating the conditions and circumstances of our lives and manifesting our future in front of our very eyes. Within the seed of individual thoughts, lie the origins of the causes we create in our reality. In fact, our thoughts give meaning to our experience of reality, which is why each of us holds a different perspective of the world around us. Remember that thought creates causes. Thought gives meaning to circumstances. Thoughts are creatively manifesting our reality.

The following questions help us gain greater clarity about our thought processes, allowing us to find the answers that will enable us to activate, energize, and profit from the Law of Attraction and to achieve the success we desire in life:

- How are my thoughts causing, creating, and maintaining my current life circumstances?
- How can I begin interpreting my world differently?
- How can I change my patterns of thinking?
- How can I model other people's successful behaviors, habits, decisions, thoughts, and actions?

Our life experience reflects our thought manifestations. The unerring Law of Attraction confirms that each of us will automatically attract the exact reward that we have earned.

We will succeed if we keep vigorously and enthusiastically attempting to activate, energize, and profit from the Law of Attraction.

INSIGHT & INSPIRATION

"SELF-CONTROL IS STRENGTH. RIGHT THOUGHT IS MASTERY. CALMNESS IS POWER."

JAMES ALLEN

THE POWER OF SELF-CONTROL

Power steering is a marvelous invention. I remember as a boy the first time my mother drove a car with power steering. As she went to turn onto the road, inexperienced with the ease of power steering, she turned too abruptly and ran into a neighbor's fence. The ease of control she had was overwhelming. A single finger can control a 300-horsepower engine in a vehicle traveling at any speed. Wouldn't it be incredible if we had the same control over our thinking?

We have great authority over our physical selves. If we want to bend our finger, our finger will bend. Our legs move merely at the suggestion of our thought. Of course, this authority has varying degrees of control. We basically have complete control over our fingers but little or no control over our heart or liver. If we want to close our eyes, they close, but if we want to stop our heart from beating, the heart pays no attention to us. Somewhere between these two extremes lies the power of our self-control.

Self-control involves directing, restraining, or governing our influence. We can exercise direction, restraint, motivation, and government over our organs, our capabilities, our emotions, and our behaviors; and the ultimate self-control would be to achieve a sort of fingertip power steering arrangement so that all our faculties and inclinations respond to our slightest touch. Our thoughts, natures, and ideas would then never run wild, nor would our emotions get out of control. Our ability to activate, energize, and profit from the Law of Attraction would be uncontainable.

The greatest accomplishment is to train the mind to extend and increase its authority over the physical circumstances of our lives. Real life is probably the best place to teach ourselves self-control. Life is also the place where we are most highly rewarded for the development of self-mastery.

One of the first steps toward self-control is planning. Every day we should sit down and plan and think and analyze and reason. We should make a program for the activities of the day, but also, we should build up our morale and decide how and what our thinking will be for that day — what events, circumstances, or other manifestations are we going to direct with our thoughts.

Follow up is also extremely important. We should never give anyone an assignment and then not check up on them. It is even more dangerous with us. We should develop the absolute best methods to motivate, restrain, and guide ourselves in directing our thinking toward our desired outcome.

Do not become too discouraged if this influence and control takes time to complete. No idea is ever born fully symmetrical, well formed, with maximum power or polish. It is a part of subsequent growth and development.

Self-control exercised over our thinking is the most effective road to success, power, and happiness.

Insight & Inspiration

"GENTLE PERSUATION SUCCEEDS WHERE FORCE FAILS."

AESOP

THE PERSUASION PRINCIPLE

Sometimes the hardest person to convince is oneself. The persuasion principle is one of the greatest powers in the universe. The dictionary says that "persuasion is to win over, by entreaty, reasoning, or by an appeal; to recommend for acceptance, to allure, convince, impel, induce, lead or move. To persuade is to bring the will of another to a desired decision by some influence short of compulsion." But persuasion may also mean to win over and convince our own minds.

For instance, if we are not convinced that Utah has the greatest snow on earth, it is unlikely that we would bother traveling there to go skiing. Persuasion is dependent on conviction. If we are unconvinced that the Law of Attraction is effective, it will be impossible to persuade our thinking to manifest our desires.

Politicians, ministers, salesmen and others rely heavily

on persuasion and many of the world's great advancements came by way of the persuasion principle. It's hard to imagine but the automobile was at first considered inferior to the horse and was met with resistance. People had to be persuaded and sold on the idea of a horseless carriage.

Here are some things to remember when persuading yourself that you have the power to activate, energize, and profit from the Law of Attraction:

Clarity. Be sure of what you want. Have a clear and solid image of what you desire to manifest in your life. Vacillating between different possibilities only sets up confusion. Get the exact sense, exactly the right shading, of what you intend to manifest.

Understanding. You must know your mind and heart. What are your principles and values, what do you love, and what affinity do your desires have with the objects of your manifestations?

Pleasure. Will the object of your desired manifestation bring you pleasure? The persuasion principle consists as much in pleasing as in convincing. We are persuaded by 'likes' more than by logic.

Conviction. We must be convinced in our ability to manifest our desires. Belief is an all-important element in the persuasion principle.

Expression. We must be able to effectively express the

desires and ideas we feel to the Universe and to our own subconscious understanding.

The persuasion principle is the power to enlighten, to convince, to produce action, and to profit from the Law of Attraction. The power of persuasion is one of the greatest powers ever placed in our hands.

INSIGHT & INSPIRATION

"ALL PASSIONS EXAGGERATE; AND THEY ARE PASSIONS ONLY BECAUSE THEY EXAGGERATE."

NICHOLAS CHAMFORT

THE POWER OF EXAGGERATION

Life, with its contrasting elements and challenging consequence, can be funny at times. There are formulas for success—they are exact and unchanging. Prescriptions for personal growth and achievement can be put down on paper, but human success and accomplishment are not that simple. Sometimes people succeed and we cannot explain their success. Others fail where all indications say they should have succeeded.

The personality traits that determine our success have been included by Creation for a healthful purpose, though we may not recognize the purpose they serve. For example, the trait of exaggeration is, it would seem, an undesirable trait and yet so many of us exaggerate constantly. A quality so prominent in human nature must have been put there for a good purpose.

The power of exaggeration is extremely beneficial

when its constructive purpose is understood. This natural tendency in human beings to exaggerate shows up early in life. Children usually live in a beautiful imaginary world where things are enlarged or connected by them to suit their convenience, and the parents and homes of the children are given an important magnificence that can lift them up.

When we compare our own children with others, it is natural to see our children as cuter, smarter, or somehow better than anyone else's. Isn't it strange that everyone in the world is great and good and fair in the eyes of some people though they may be extremely small and undesirable in the eyes of others? That usually involves some exaggeration beyond the ordinary.

Because Nature has provided us with the powerful ability to see things in different lights, according to our interests, the mind becomes all-powerful. The power of exaggeration, as John Milton observed, can make a heaven of hell or a hell of heaven. Imagine the thrill and excitement the ability to exaggerate could give to what would otherwise be an ordinary existence.

Too often, the importance of life is painted in drab colors and life's music is tuned down to seem ordinary and unexciting. The power of exaggeration together with a vivid imagination helps us paint pictures and dream dreams that correspond with our hopes. We need the ability to look at our world through rose-colored glasses and to envision an exaggerated existence that is filled with our personal desires.

Much of life's success consists in knowing which things to exaggerate and which to reduce in size. In other words, through which end of the telescope should we examine our lives? We often look at our challenges, faults, and trials through the magnifying end, seeing them exaggerated beyond proportion. Our blessings, abilities, and benefits we tend to see through the opposite end of the telescope, making them tiny and insignificant. How wonderful life would seem if we reversed the view. The affective, judicious use of the ability to enlarge our benefits and reduce our problems is probably the greatest single source of happiness.

The power of exaggeration gives us super-picturing power and the ability to enlarge our visualization, making our inner images more intense and meaningful. It allows colorful visions and angelic music to surround us. This quality enables the most unassuming person to see their objectives and desires multiplied in magnificence and enlarged in attraction.

Some may feel that to deliberately change the size of things we present in our minds and emotions is a form of misrepresentation. It is not. The apostle Paul taught, "for now we see through a glass, darkly." [33] The power of exaggeration helps us to lighten things up and see them as they will at some time actually be.

The power to exaggerate is a great human ability and knowing when to reverse the telescope is like painting a great picture; it's a fine art. It is one of the greatest good fortunes of

---

[33] 1 Corinthians 13:13.

our lives that we may enlarge to our hearts' content the importance of those things that are good for us and will bring us happiness and blot out our attention to those things that otherwise would draw us down.

Insight & Inspiration

"A MIND, ONCE EXPANDED BY A NEW IDEA, NEVER RETURNS TO ITS ORIGINAL DIMENSIONS."

OLIVER WENDELL HOLMES

THE INCREASING RETURNS PRINCIPLE

We live in a world governed by laws. We can become the beneficiaries of every one of these laws. One of the greatest of all laws and one that we frequently overlook is the law of increasing returns.

In technical terms, we would define the principle of increasing returns by explaining that an increase of labor or capital applied beyond a certain point causes a greater than proportionate increase in production. In simpler terms, the person that works 10% harder, in the right way, should produce 20, 30, 50, or even 100% more.

Let me illustrate it this way: I am offering you twenty-nine tools to improve your ability to activate, energize, and profit from the Law of Attraction. This can seem overwhelming, I know. So, let's suppose you are implementing only six of these 29 principles and powers of attraction. And let's suppose that, on a scale of 1 to 5, you rated a 3 on each of these principles. Your score, or your ability to manifest, would look like this:

$$3 \times 3 \times 3 \times 3 \times 3 \times 3 = 729$$

Then suppose that by improvement you could increase your ability and rating to a 4. Your total improvement wouldn't be 1 x 6 but instead:

$$4 \times 4 \times 4 \times 4 \times 4 \times 4 = 4,096.$$

You would increase each principle or power by only 1 and yet the total result is increased over 5 times. In other words, you don't need to be twice as good at utilizing the Law of Attraction. If you are one third better, your score maybe five times as great.

I once asked my daughter if she would rather have a penny doubled every day for a month, or a one-time payment of $10,000. She chose the $10,000. Of course, she was too young to realize or understand that a penny doubled every day for thirty days would equal $10,737,418.24. Add just one more day and it would be $21,474,836.48.

Doing even a little more each day brings substantial returns. Some people do as little as they possibly can to get by and that is about all that they ever do get. A coworker of mine used to say, "I do just enough work so that they don't fire me, and they pay me just enough money so that I don't quit." If we approach the Law of Attraction with that attitude, we will have exceptionally little success manifesting our desires.

In school, 70% is a passing grade. If we worked hard enough to get 69%, we failed; but if we studied enough to get 71%, we passed. What a tremendous difference was made by that small extra effort. However, if we worked a little more effectively still, we could make it to 100%. This small additional effort at the top of the scale can make all the difference in achieving our desires. If one person is just a little more thoughtful, plans a little better, works a little harder, stays at it a little longer, studies a little more, then that person receives several times more than another.

In the movie, *The Razor's Edge*, there were eight starring actors and eight stand-ins to do the hard, grueling, tiresome work. The stand in for Tyrone Powers was Thomas Noonan, a close associate. They had gone to high school together. They were about the same size, equally intelligent, and were remarkably similar in appearance. But in one way, they were not similar. The stars may have been a little bit better, but their salary was 75% higher than the stand-ins'.

One of the greatest lessons of attraction is to go the extra mile. Do a little more and do it with a little more faith, a little more energy, a little more devotion, a little more determination, and we will have transformed ourselves from a stand-in to a star. The difference is just a little improvement in attitude and a little more effort in the right direction. The results are tremendous though the difference may be as fine as a razor's edge.

Insight & Inspiration

"WHAT YOU THINK YOU BECOME. WHAT YOU FEEL YOU ATTRACT. WHAT YOU IMAGINE YOU CREATE."

BUDDHA

THE POWER OF ATTRACTION

An old Chinese custom provided that if you visit a Chinese home and you greatly admire some item you see there, the homeowner will give it to you as a gift. Isn't that exactly what life also does to us? The power of the fundamental Law of Attraction provides that that which we love, admire, and desire, we receive. The power of attraction creates our character, our friends, our abilities as well as our material possessions.

In his book, *Law of Attraction*, Michael J. Lozier, tells us that "the law of attraction will respond to your vibration whether positive or negative in giving you more of what you were vibrating." [34]

This is one of the most powerful of all laws governing the development of our characters and personality. If properly understood and developed, it has a tremendous value.

---

[34] Lozier, Michael J., *Law of Attraction*, pg. 14.

Michael J. Lousier defines the Law of Attraction as bringing into our life whatever we give our energy, focus, and attention to, whether wanted or unwanted.

The power of attraction isn't just a fancy term or New Age magic; it is a law of Nature. Every atom of our minds and bodies is constantly responding to this law whether we know it or not. The Law of Attraction responds to whatever vibration we are offering, by giving us more of what we are vibrating.

Everyone gives off vibrations. Some of us give off good vibes, others give off bad vibes. The power of attraction doesn't decide whether our desires are good for us or not, it simply responds to our vibration.

We are constantly vibrating. If we are excited, content, appreciative, or feeling gratitude or pride, then we are offering positive vibrations. If we are angry, sad, disappointed, or feeling poor, unlucky, or defeated, then we are sending out negative vibrations. We will activate, energize, and either profit or lose through the power of attraction.

Whatever we are vibrating, the power of attraction will increase for us. Most of the time, we are unaware of the vibrations we are offering. The power of attraction simply responds to whatever we are vibrating by giving us more of that feeling.

INSIGHT & INSPIRATION

"YOU HAVE THE CAPABILITY TO CHANGE YOUR LIFE ALL WITH A SIMPLE SHIFT IN PERSPECTIVE."

DEMI LOVATO

THE PERSPECTIVE PRINCIPLE

The perspective principle is the provision that makes everything close appear large and important while everything far away seems small and insignificant. For instance, on January 12th Tax Day may not seem as alarming and urgent as it does on April 12th.

Standing on a street corner looking down a long row of telephone poles, the pole closest to us seems especially tall and impressive while the one in the distance is barely an insignificant pinpoint. Our eyes tell us that this is reality, but if we were to drive to the horizon and look back, we would discover that the tall, impressive telephone pole had become insignificant and small and that the one next to us, which seemed of no consequence at the time, is now the most impressive of them all.

The perspective principle emphasizes the fact that things are not always as they seem. Life is fraught with optical illusions which sight cannot detect nor reason comprehend. From our perspective the earth appears flat. The sun seems to revolve around us and not us around the sun. In many instances in life, our senses and reason are useless.

Oftentimes we frantically concern ourselves about difficulties and dilemmas which, because of our nearness to them, have an importance all out of proportion to fact. Likewise, we often give little or no importance at all to something that lies in the distance of either time or space. The sun has a diameter of 866 thousand miles but an insignificant coin the size of a quarter will obstruct our vision of this enormous star if we place the coin close enough to our eyes.

Activating, energizing, and profiting from the Law of Attraction requires that we learn that certain impressions and evidence must be weighed and shaded in their proper perspective. When we begin a project of manifesting any worthwhile desire in life, little problems we run up against often appear monumental in size. The thought of achieving and living those desires and grand accomplishments appears so distant it seems to hold little current consequence. Looking back from the horizon of life, we will then know that the telephone pole that we thought insignificant has now become by far the most important of them all.

A discouraged student in any discipline may find it difficult to see far enough down the road to appreciate the influence of current circumstances on future results. The deception of perspective makes us short-sighted but, in the end, the little problems and difficulties we experience at the beginning in activating, energizing, and profiting from the Law of Attraction, we will no longer remember except in amazement that we ever gave them a second thought.

The perspective principle can best be illustrated by the story of the six blind men from Indostan who went to see an elephant. One took hold of the elephant's tail and discerned that an elephant is like a rope. One felt the broad side of the elephant and decided an elephant is like a wall. Another stood by the elephant's leg and determined that an elephant is like a tree. One took hold of his trunk and thought an elephant is like a snake. One felt the animal's tusk and determined that an elephant is like a spear. And finally, one took hold of the ear and decided that an elephant is like a fan. Their point of view, or perspective, gave each an entirely different impression of this unique and marvelous creature. None of them were completely wrong in their perception, but none of them were entirely right.

The long perspective is remarkable. Its effect on the attitude, enjoyment, and appreciation we feel in our manifestation efforts is heartening. While we are holding on to the elephant's tail, the perspective principle helps us develop the ability to see clearly that the elephant also has a trunk. While we attempt to activate, energize, and profit from the Law of Attraction, we should remember that things are not always as they seem.

The world is not as flat as it appears. It is not standing still as it may seem to us but is hurtling through space at tremendous speed. The people we associate with are not small and inconsiderate while we are big and generous. The sun is not smaller than a quarter. The telephone pole on the horizon is not as inconsequential as it seems; it is, in fact, the biggest telephone pole in the entire system.

INSIGHT & INSPIRATION

"I AM LOOKING OUT THROUGH THE LIBRARY WINDOW INTO THE APPLE ORCHARD, AND I SEE MILLIONS OF BLOSSOMS THAT WILL NEVER MATERIALIZE AND BECOME FRUIT FOR LACK OF VITALIZATION."

ELBURT HUBBARD

THE POWER OF SELF-SUPERVISION

It is an oddity of the human personality that only a relatively few people ever learn to direct their own efforts according to their own previously thought-out plans.

Being able to affect our lives through the Law of Attraction skillfully and correctly is meaningful and important, and yet that is probably the smallest part of our achievement. The effort of visualizing, affirming, and manifesting our desires isn't the hindrance that's holding us back; it's learning to supervise and motivate ourselves—to think positively, to organize our train of thought, and to execute our designs on our own.

Tragically, (as I stated earlier), when left to their own devices, most people either sit down, lie down, or fall down. The executive portion of their personalities becomes nonproductive. Their initiative and their ability to persist in their efforts seem to evaporate from their minds.

Bing cherry trees are incapable of producing fruit if left by themselves. They have no fertilizing pollen, and so a pollinizer must be planted among them. Then the wind and the bees carry the pollen to those trees that are incapable of self-fertilization. People are often like that when it comes to self-motivation. We may be extremely skilled at using our mental abilities to manifest our desires but unless we are self-motivated our initiative, abilities, and planning will remain unproductive.

Studies have shown that if a company has a task that requires five employees to complete it, it will be accomplished more rapidly and effectively if one of the five is assigned as supervisor and held responsible for keeping the other four busy and working.

In business, the amount of supervision a person requires largely determines what he or she is worth. A person who requires substantial supervision cannot expect much pay while one who requires a little less supervision gets a little larger income. When that employee can be depended upon to complete the task without any supervision, he or she is worth even more. At the top of the pay grade are those who do their own work, on their own initiative, following their own plans which they themselves have devised and initiated.

The destiny of a cherry blossom is that it should become a cherry, and the destiny of a human soul is that it may become God-like. But neither of these things happen unless that vitalizing element is introduced that makes us productive.

In the process of training ourselves to activate, energize, and profit from the Law of Attraction, we must not forget the importance of learning to stand on our own feet, supply our own ideas, develop our own initiative, and motivate our own thinking.

Successful manifestation lies largely in the ability to mentally discipline ourselves. One of the most exalting feelings we will ever know is the feeling that we are bigger than circumstance and that we can manifest the innermost desires of our hearts against all obstacles. We reach this point by learning something that most people never discover: the power of self-supervision. We are then bigger than anything that can happen to us.

INSIGHT & INSPIRATION

"IF YOU WANT TO DEVELOP A STRONG BACK, GET A HEAVY LOAD TO CARRY."

UNKNOWN

THE GROWTH PRINCIPLE

Life is made up of opposites. Our motivation is the method used to overcome inertia. The growth principle is a principle of struggle. It is the process of overcoming obstacles.

The power to grow is the power to struggle. Suppose that all our objectives in life could be immediately realized. Suppose that all the races could be won, and all progress could be completely affected and recorded at this very instant. There would be great joy and happiness now, but the future would probably be filled with boredom and discontent.

Happiness comes while we are in pursuit of our most important dreams and desires. We often do not seek things for themselves alone, but for the joy we have in the search.

How much interest would we have in a mystery novel if 'who-done-it' was spelled out for us on the very first page?

In a play, each scene preceding the climax arouses the emotions of challenging accomplishment at the end. Discovering the end without the journey destroys the intrigue of the play.

Those who do not persist in struggle do not grow. The only way that anyone has ever been known to coast is downhill. The reason the grass looks greener on the other side of the fence is because Nature is trying to entice us forward. It is attempting to stimulate our appetite for the chase. It is trying to intrigue us not to give up the fight.

We have been given a restlessness in our natures. We want to get something a little better. We drop one thing as soon as it has been attained and start pursuing something else. We have been given an upward reach; this ability to grow constitutes the God-like instinct that the Universe has planted within us.

Life is a climb up the mountain. We start at the bottom and just when we appear to be at the top, we discover that we are only at the top of the first ascent. From this level, we see another length of mountain reaching above and beyond it. Similarly, when we accomplish anything, we always see a new objective spreading itself ahead of us. It is our nature never to be fully satisfied.

If we keep this climbing characteristic within us active, we are safe. We should constantly be stimulating ourselves. Physical stimulants can be harmful, but mental and spiritual stimulants are necessary for growth, and the more habit forming they are the better. A part of the growth principle implies that if we are not going forward, we will slip backward. When we stop being better, we stop being good.

No matter what limitation, inadequacy, or deficiency we may have, if we just keep moving in the right direction we may hope to someday arrive at our destination, and everything will turn out alright.

INSIGHT & INSPIRATION

"IF WE ARE GRATEFUL FOR SOMETHING THAT WE DON'T YET HAVE, IT WILL SHOW UP."

BILL WYLSON

GEM TWENTY-NINE

THE POWER OF APPRECIATION

Appreciation in advance is one of the greatest affirmations available to us. Being appreciative for manifestations that have not yet materialized is an act of faith. It comes from knowing that when we ask, we shall receive. In effect, we are saying "thank you" for something we have yet to receive. The power of appreciation delivers our deepest desires to us.

We have established by now that everything we receive comes by the Law of Attraction. In expressing appreciation for what we don't have but desire, we are projecting a thought that can bring about the realization of our desire. In his book, *Law of Attraction*, Michael J. Losier reveals that "appreciation and gratitude are the highest forms of vibration." [35] As I stated earlier in this book, grateful appreciation in advance for the manifestation of our desires is one of the best tricks to play on the subconscious.

---

[35] Losier, Michael J., *Law of Attraction*, p. 80.

Thankfulness and appreciation confirm to the subconscious that it needs to conform to the reality of our gratitude in a hurry. The subconscious mind does not take into consideration time or space. It can only comprehend the present moment. It is important to affirm and visualize goals as already completed in the present. It is equally important to be appreciative for those things you desire even before you have received them.

When we develop a sincere expression of appreciativeness for all that we have been given, we are, in effect, opening the channels to receive even more. Appreciation is a thought pattern strongly tied to an emotion and it will take root, blossoming eventually into acts, events, and circumstances that will bear the fruit of opportunity and abundance. Our feelings, more than the words we think or say to ourselves, are the real language that the Law of Attraction responds to. If our words are divorced from our emotions, then our petition to the Universe has no real power. It sits like a lead weight, never rising to the fulfillment of the spoken desire.

Appreciation creates energy. It helps us focus on the positive and draws us away from the negative. When we are grateful for something, we are offering a feeling and vibration of pure joy. Taking time to purposely treasure every day means that we are intentionally offering pure, strong, positive vibrations. In that same moment, the Law of Attraction is unfolding to bring us more of what we are vibrating.

Appreciation is a beneficial feeling with a particular therapeutic power. But thankfulness easily slips away from us. If we don't look deep into ourselves and admit how much we need the power of appreciation we lose the benefit of what being thankful will bring to us.

Just as words without feeling are powerless to help us manifest our desires, emotion without thought has no direction and will never find its intended target. When we link thought and emotion, words and feelings together, like a bow and arrow, then our desires take off to meet their target with speed and accuracy. Manifestation is the result of both elements working in harmony.

Being appreciative means giving a fullness of thanks. Giving thanks is an outward expression of a grateful heart. Appreciation is the feeling within our heart. Be thankful for everything you have in life. Say "thank you" for each breath.

As I stated previously, if we are thankful for anything in life, we might as well be thankful for everything, good and bad, positive and negative. All the events, circumstances, and conditions which have occurred were necessary to bring us where we are today. We should accept all incidences and manifestations as positive steps on the path toward the achievement of our desires.

Sincere appreciation is conveyed through action. Honest appreciativeness implies more than just a feeling in the heart. Grateful appreciation implies demonstrating gratitude by giving. We demonstrate heartfelt thankfulness through offering kind gestures, listening ears, and open hearts to anyone in need. Giving thanks means *living* thanks. Ann Monroe Lindbergh said it this way: "One can never pay in gratitude; one can only pay in-kind somewhere else in life."

To be filled with the power of appreciation is one of the most important principles for receiving the manifestation of our desires. We should give thanks for whatever gifts have manifested in our lives. When we receive all things with thankfulness, we put ourselves into a position to receive even more, for which we should be even more grateful. If we are grateful for what we already have, we will receive more. It is impossible to overdo gratitude.

James Twyman states that "the closest we can come to divine love is by being in a state of gratitude. If we all developed the habit of counting our blessings, even though it seemed so basic or old-fashioned, then we would be so grateful for our life that we would actually attract love."

INSIGHT & INSPIRATION

"LIFE IS ALL ABOUT BEING TRUE TO YOURSELF AND WHAT YOU BELIEVE IN."

ANDY BIERSACK

THE TRUE BUSINESS OF LIFE

What is the great question of life? It is the question: "Why am I here? What is the purpose of my life?" This question is the foundation for the development of all philosophies. It is the question behind all religion. Even the scientist, looking to unlock the laws governing the ever-unfolding universe asks: "Why am I?" This is the question of all people everywhere throughout all time.

Obstacles to finding right responses to this question arise when we look for the answer outside of ourselves, especially when, not finding it, we gradually begin to ignore the question altogether.

In *Law of Attraction,* Michael J. Lozier suggests that the purpose of life is to know and experience complete joy. The answer to finding the purpose of our existence is simple and straight-forward when we look within ourselves. Each one of us is individually and intimately connected to the Omnipotent, Omniscient and Omnipresent. Our consciousness is part of the Universal Consciousness. When we search within ourselves, entering the silence and allowing the Infinite to flow through us, we discover our own singular answer.

When we accept who we truly are, the answer is obvious. We are the individual channel through which the Infinite expresses itself.

As I explained in *The Power of Attraction*, our free-will to choose empowers and enables us to create. What we choose to create can glorify Infinite Intelligence. What we choose to create can contribute to the continuous expression of a constantly unfolding cosmos. The answer is delivered to us through inspiration which, like fine-tuning a radio for perfect reception of our favorite station, is simply the art of adjusting the individual mind to that of the Universal Mind. We become a channel for the flow of infinite wisdom.

All great things come through recognition. The scepter of power is consciousness and thought is its messenger. This messenger is constantly forming the realities of the invisible world of thought into the conditions and environments of our objective world. Thinking is the true business of life and power is the result. We are constantly and continuously involved with the mystical and miraculous power of thought and consciousness.

The essence of the Universal is within you. When you perceive this reality, you begin to feel your own power and you begin to act; to do things. This perception gives vitality to thought. It is the fuel that fires the imagination.

You are an agent of visualization. Imagination is your workshop. Thought is creative vibration and the quality of the conditions you create will depend on the quality of your thought. Every time you think you start a train of causation which will create a condition in strict accordance with the quality of thought which originated it.

The Universal acts through the individual. We are the channel of this activity. It is within us. Become the mechanism through which the Creative acts.

Be more.
Do more.
Have more.

About the Author

Steven Claysen was born in Columbus, Ohio. As a young boy he began studying the power of thought after reading James Allen's classic little book, *As a Man Thinketh.* He became an avid reader and student of creative thinking. Steven used the power of creative thinking to improve his relationships, find the right jobs, and create wealth.

He is the founder of *DeepEnd Enterprises*, a third-tier marketing company. He also worked as a debt consultant and financial advisor at *Boardwalk Financial Services*.

www.stevenclaysen.com

www.ingramcontent.com/pod-product-compliance
Lightning Source LLC
Chambersburg PA
CBHW070350070426
42446CB00050BA/2786